Stories and Lore of the
Zodiac

Stories and

Illustrations by
ANNE BEVANS

Lore of the
Zodiac

BY
M. A. JAGENDORF

The Vanguard Press, Inc.
New York

To

Gisela Gresser and Harry Star,

two stellar intellects who have

brought many rich hours into my life.

Designer: Tom Bevans

Table of Contents

Preface

Many books have been and still are being written about the stars, but one rarely finds one so informative, so delightfully written, and as charming as this small volume by Moritz Jagendorf on the twelve signs of the zodiac. The stars are natural objects about which to weave fanciful stories, but one does not have to invent such stories today, for every civilization has contributed its share of such tales to the store of man's literature. Since these stories have stood the test of time very well and appeal to us as strongly now as to those who came before us, an astronomy book built around them is bound to make good reading, particularly when written with the loving, tender care Dr. Jagendorf brings to his task.

Although Greek mythology has given us the richest collections of stories about the constellations, Mr. Jagendorf has not limited himself to these, but has used material from the Hebrews, the Chinese, the American Indians, and the Mayans as well. But he has limited himself to the twelve, constellations that form the signs of the zodiac (the Greek word meaning "circle of animals") because these constellations lie along the ecliptic, the great circle in the sky along which the sun appears to shift its position eastwardly from day to day. The particular sign of the zodiac in which the sun happens to lie when spring begins is not the same year after year; there is a slow westward change that shifts the springtime position of the sun to a new sign of the zodiac about every two thousand years. Since this played an important role in formulating ancient man's ideas about cosmology, he invented the most interesting myths about these twelve constellations, and Dr. Jagendorf has tied them up very nicely with informative astronomical data about these signs of the zodiac.

LLOYD MOTZ
Professor of Astronomy
Columbia University
New York, N.Y.

Foreword

Do you remember the warm summer nights when you lay on your back following the racing moon among the swiftly shifting clouds? Or watching, tensely, on frosty winter nights, the sea of ever-changing stars?

I remember well those deep blue nights in my early life and the magic they brought me. They set my mind and fantasy working. So I dreamed many dreams, eyes wide open, waiting for the sharp bugle notes that came every night from the not-far-off soldier barracks calling the men to come home.

All this happened when as a boy I lived in a fine city in Austria, the capital of a province known then as Bucovina.

When I grew older and began studying about the

stars, I learned that even thousands of years ago men and perhaps young folks like you and me had done the same thing. They, too, had gazed at the stars on deep blue nights and dreamed many dreams, especially about a particular group or belt or circle of stars called the zodiac, the subject of this book.

I will tell you first a little about the great science of astronomy, the scientific study of stars. I hope it will inspire you to study more of this wonderful field of learning.

With it I will tell you something about astrology— the study and belief begun thousands of years ago by those who hold that the stars in the zodiac have a definite influence on every act of a person's life. For many people this belief is as alive today as it was before writing began.

Finally, I will tell you stories connected with the zodiac—stories from many lands and famous throughout the world for endless years.

At the end of the book you will find a list of other books that will help you study more of these subjects. Happy reading and happy learning!

M. A. Jagendorf

In the Beginning

Come with me and look at the stars, and come with me and listen to some tales about them. Just as there are stars without end, so are there tales about them without end. They are beautiful and rich and varied: stories, history, legends, poems from far and near. Star symbols and motifs filled not only stories but were also used in all the arts. Such records are found on clay tablets, stone walls, and architectural relics.

But heaven is vast, vaster than the ocean or the earth. So I will take you to only one part of the great blue sky—a part famous in all the world for thousands and thousands of years, down to the very minute you are reading these words. I mean the star realm called the zodiac: the world calendar of the sky.

What is the zodiac? Who discovered it? What did it tell and mean to those star students of old and what does it mean even to the world today?

In ancient Greek, *zoidiakos*, the word from which the word *zodiac* is derived, means a "circle of animals." The very fact that the Greeks used this word was an indication that star students, even before the Greeks, had developed the whole system of the famous "circle" in the sky. For the zodiac is a circle or belt in the heavens consisting of twelve constellations, each one exactly a thirty-degree sector of that circle, spaced all along the paths of the sun, the moon, and the planets. Within this circle in the sky these bodies have passed in periodic movements from time unknown to this very day.

The discovery of the zodiacal circle of stars is ascribed to different peoples: the Chaldeans, the Babylonians, and the Egyptians. Different groups of scholars uphold different claims, but most believe the Chaldean-Babylonians were the first to observe the orderly movements of the zodiacal constellations.

In very ancient days the Chaldeans and the Babylonians were two separate states, and though their people spoke the same language, the two were constantly battling each other. In the end the Babylonians overcame the Chaldeans, the peoples became intermingled, and from then on they were called Babylonians.

Among ancient star scholars, there was great argument. Some believed in a solar (sun) zodiac and some in a lunar (moon) zodiac—even though both sides agreed on the relationship of either system to "time." (It is interesting to note that reckoning by the moon came before reckoning by the sun.) When the star gazers—sometimes students, sometimes priests—noted the regularity of the movements of the stars and the moon, they undoubtedly began to use these movements as a measuring device. They divided them to fit the activities of their daily lives. For how important to existence is the measuring of time!

When to plant, when to reap, when to work, when to rest, when to expect rain, when to worship! The sky was their calendar, their clock.

The majority of the star students, called astronomers, observed that the sun took about twelve full-moon periods to make its circle around the heavens, and thus the year's time began its division into twelve months.

This number twelve was an important figure in ancient days. There were twelve archangels and twelve apostles, twelve tribes of Israel and twelve sheaves of wheat in Joseph's dream. The high priest in Jerusalem had on his breastplate twelve different precious stones. Hercules performed twelve difficult tasks.

For some reason the Egyptian astronomers found it simpler to divide the year by groups of stars that appeared to them regularly every ten days (most of these groups were in the zodiacal circle). So they divided the circular movement of the heavenly bodies into tens—called decans.

Originally the decans were not divisions of the zodiac. That came later, when the ancient Egyptians divided the movement of the sun, the moon, and stars into thirty-six decans—ten-day periods that gave them 360 days for the year.

But probably the star gazers very soon saw that 360 days did not make a full year in accordance with the heavenly bodies; more days were needed than the decans totaled. So these observers added five days to the beginning of each year and one more every four years to make the leap year.

The next scientific study was the division into the

four astronomical seasons: spring, summer, fall, and winter, each set in a quarter part of the zodiacal circle. Thus it was this heaven-star division that gave us the measurement of the year's time: not only the weeks and months, but the seasons as well.

But the star students saw much more in the gleaming heavenly bodies. They gazed up high, nights without end, and in the constant gazing the shimmery moving stars took on for them unusual forms and a great, strange life.

This was only natural. When you look at moving clouds in the sky, they do take on different shapes—now animals, now humans, now fish, now grotesque figures. The more the ancient star gazers looked, the more definite the shapes seemed to them. These forms—animals, humans, and objects—seemed far more than mere animals, humans, and objects; they were alive and had superpowers. They had meaning, life. They were high out of reach. A ram . . . a goat . . . a fish . . . a bull, lion . . . crab . . . figures of humans . . . even scales. Surely they must be gods! They must be the great power high above all! High above the earth, directing time, the seasons, and, unquestionably to them, man's life—his health, his destiny. In those ancient days the stars were part of the religions of much of the known world, accepted almost universally. Cleopatra, the great queen of Egypt, traveled with her private astrologer. Roman emperors had their own astrologers at court. By the fifth century B.C. faith in the zodiac was part of the daily life of the Greeks and Romans. As time went on, the Church tried to stop this belief, but with no success. Often, Church dignitaries themselves had their own personal astrologers, and universities had special departments for the study of astrology. To this day, among the Chinese and Japanese, animal symbols are assigned to years, months, days, and even hours.

With the years, this faith and scope in the power of the stars continued to grow. There were even popular rhymes about the zodiac. Here is one that was well known:

The ram and the bull lead the line.
Next, twins and crab and lion shine.
The virgin and the scales,
Scorpion and archer next are due.
Goat and water-bearer too.
And fish with glittering tails.

Not only were the twelve signs divided into four seasons but also into four "elements": earth, water, fire, and air. These were called the four trigons, and each trigon contained three divisions of the zodiac:

Fire (hot and dry); the fiery trigon contained
    Aries, Leo, Sagittarius.
Earth (cold and dry); the earthly trigon contained
    Taurus, Virgo, Capricornus.
Water (cold and wet); the watery trigon contained
    Cancer, Scorpio, Pisces.
Air (hot and wet); the airy trigon contained
    Gemini, Libra, Aquarius.

The zodiac was also considered magic: black magic foretelling tragedy, sorrow, deadly sickness, and great misfortune; white magic foretelling good fortune and joys.

The zodiac was also connected with the Bible: Aries

the Ram was God; Cancer was Benjamin; Leo was Judah, and so on. Every Israelite tribe was represented by a sign in the zodiac.

Astrology also reached into medicine. Stars were believed to have power over different parts of the body, and medical treatment was given according to the mystic connection between certain stars and particular parts of the body. Capricornus was thought to influence the knee; Taurus the bull, the neck; Aries the Ram, the head. Cancer was believed to be the doctor for the hard part of the chest; and Libra to care for both sides as far down as the hands reach, and so on. Even philosophers of medieval days supported these claims.

So common and so serious was the belief in the influence of the zodiac on the body that popular rhymes were made about it, like this one:

The Head and the Face the princely Ram doth Rule,
The Neck and Throat falls to the sullen Bull,
The lovely Twins guard Shoulder, Arm and Hand,
The slow-paced Crab doth Breast and Spleen command.
The Lion bold governs the Heart of man.
The Modest Maid doth of the Bowels scan,
The Reins and Loins are in the Balance tried,
The Scorpion the secret parts doth guide.
The Shooting Horse lays claim to both the Thighs;
The Knees upon the headstrong Goat relies.
The Waterman, the both legs doth claim.
The Fishes rule the feet and meet the Ram again.

The stars also were thought to rule man's sentiments

and emotions. If you were born under Aries, it was claimed you were fierce and vital; those born under Taurus were thought to have practical understanding for common things; while those born under Gemini were said to be intellectual. There was not a nook or cranny of life about which it was believed the zodiac did not have a definite influence.

In short, the zodiacal constellations, astrology, and horoscopes (the doctrine that the position of the stars at one's birth foretells one's whole destiny) entered into every part of home and health from the years far, far behind us through medieval times, and in many ways to the very present. Of course, with the discoveries and growth of modern science, much of the belief in this influence has disappeared, but not all.

Today, the true meaning of the zodiac to astronomers is as important as it was thousands of years ago. And to a large extent the belief in astrology, so closely related to the zodiac, is still held by millions. Horoscopes flourish wherever winds blow and stars shine. And this includes the United States of America, where it is claimed by some that professional astrologers, by casting and interpreting horoscopes, earn more than fifty million dollars a year. Astrology has even been entered by the mystery of computers.

And now, having told you just a little of the history of the zodiac, let me turn to some of the tales built around the ever-gleaming zodiacal constellations.

ARIES
THE RAM

"At last from Aries rolls the boun-
teous sun."*

I will begin with Aries the Ram, leader of the host of
the zodiac and most often connected with spring.

Aries consists of a cluster of stars, three of which are

* James Thomson, *The Seasons*: "Spring" (London, 1738)

prominent, forming a triangle. The rest make a dim line going in the direction of Taurus and the Pleiades, which are also in the realm of the zodiac. The three stars and the cluster do not look like a ram, but the ancient star-gazers saw them as such, or there may have been some particular reason for calling them so.

But why was this collection of little stars chosen as the guiding group in the great zodiac in the heavens? Why were the almighty, golden god of Egypt and the high-thundering god of Greece shown to their believers in the likeness of a ram?

Here are some of the reasons why Aries has been so prominent for thousands of years, down to our time.

Some three thousand years ago there was an ancient tradition that the world was created when the sun entered the constellation of the Ram in the course of its apparent yearly movement around the earth, because this was the time of the year when the days grew longer than the nights and the sun shone warmer. It was the time when flower-footed spring came to the land, promising new life in fields and woods, and warmth to the body. For many years at that time the coming of the sun to Aries was designated as the start of the new year, with all its rich promises of abundance and joys.

So strong was belief in the stars then that man held the zodiac as master of the sun, directing its daily course. If it were not for the power of these stars, it was believed, there would be no spring, no growth on earth, no bright seasons.

So thus, to these ancients some three thousand years

ago, the year began when the sun entered the constellation of the Ram. This event was called by the astronomers "the first point of Aries." Belief in this occurrence has lasted to this very day, though now the sun is in a different constellation when spring arrives.

Probably, way back in the dimness of years, the Ram had an important meaning. What that was is not known. In ancient Hindu mythology, "Ram" means God. We know that the Egyptians worshiped the ram; their sun god Ammon had the head of a ram. The ram had a very important place in Greek life, too.

Now let me tell you what astrology says about people born under Aries: about their character and fortune. Those born from March 22 to April 20 under the "fortunate and masculine sign," under the sign of the "first fire," are thought by those who believe in astrology to be strong, full of energy and spirit, with a great vital force driving them to probe and create in many of the arts. They try to shine in public life and love music and dancing. Full of impulses, they are ever striving toward creative experimenting. Thus they are ever ready to fight for success in life.

Their faults are stubbornness and impatience and sometimes selfishness and foolish generosity. Women born under Aries are often quite jealous. But most of these faults can be overcome by patience and kindness.

Diamonds and bloodstones are the jewels of the month, and the favorite flower is the violet.

And now here is one of the world's great tales, which tells how the Ram came into the sky, into the zodiac constellation known as Aries.

The Ram with the Golden Fleece

There is a great tale told in ancient Greece of a ram with a golden fleece. Some tell the story one way, some another, and some say it is about the Ram in the constellation in the zodiac. But whatever is said about it, however the tale runs, it is worthy of being told over and over again, and here is how it goes.

There was a Greek king named Athamas who had come from Boeotia, the ancient republic north of Attica, to live in Thessaly. He was married to Nephele, who, according to legend, was a phantom created by Zeus, the greatest of the Greek gods.

They had a son named Phryxus and a daughter who was called Helle, but there was little joy between the king and queen.

Nephele was always reproaching her husband: "I

was created by the gods, but you were born of a woman just like any mortal."

"I am a king, Nephele. Men obey me as they do the gods."

"They do not. A word from the gods, and you would be destroyed."

This argument continued on and on. There was no end to the quarreling, and Athamas was very unhappy.

Often the queen stayed away from her home for weeks without thought of her children or her husband. The king grew lonesome and wretched, and so he began looking for friendship and companionship elsewhere.

One day he saw Ino, the daughter of King Cadmus, and she looked on him with friendly eyes.

"Come to my palace, Ino," he said. "My son and daughter need someone to watch over them."

So Ino came, and Helle and Phryxus liked her.

But when Nephele returned from her wanderings and saw Ino, her anger knew no bounds. A fierce rivalry grew up between the two, and they were always plotting to harm each other.

One day Nephele stormed up to Mount Olympus, the home of the gods, and complained bitterly against her husband to Hera, the wife of Zeus.

"He has brought a woman into my palace, and my children want to be with her and not with me!"

The goddess listened to her and felt sorry for her. She promised Nephele she would bring tragic vengeance on Athamas for this.

Nephele returned triumphantly to the city and demanded the death of King Athamas.

"He is cursed and condemned by the gods, and I demand his death," she cried.

But the citizens thought differently and refused the cruel request.

The queen's demand roused Ino to wild anger, and she vowed revenge. On a warm spring day she walked through the fields, and there she saw the women of the royal household sowing corn. A thought, poisoned by anger, went through her mind. She said:

"Women of the royal palace, you work hard, with little reward. And for whom? For a queen who has no regard for her husband and neglects her children. Many days she is away from them. Teach her a lesson she well deserves and I will reward you well for it. Sow old parched corn so no fresh young stalks will come up. Perhaps that will awaken her to be a good mother. Remember, I will reward you for this."

The women knew Ino's words were true, so they did what she asked. No green corn grew in the gray field.

"Why have the gods brought this misfortune on me?" cried the king. "What wrong have I done? I'll send messengers to the oracle of Delphi to learn the cause of this ill luck and do penance for it."

He sent the messengers at once, but Ino was ready and stopped them on their way.

"Men of Thessaly," she said, "you are cursed and there will be no corn for you this year. You are cursed because the queen of your land is forgetful of her husband and her children. I know what will lift this affliction from your kingdom and will bring food to the earth. Nephele does not want her son. Tell the king to sacrifice

Phryxus, the unwanted son of Nephele, to the gods, and the corn will grow with green leaves and yellow fruit. It will be for the good of your land, and I will pay you well." And right then she gave them golden coins. "Go to the king with my message and I will give you more gold."

The messengers left and soon were back to the king with the words they had been told to say: that only the sacrifice of Phryxus would bring growth to the earth.

Athamas fell into black grief, for he loved his son, and Nephele was in a wild fury. But the order of the gods had to be obeyed. Came the early morning of the fatal day, and the king, weeping bitter tears, led his handsome son to the mountaintop to be sacrificed. Among those who followed in the great mass of citizens was Heracles, the greatest hero of Greece. He rushed up to the king and shouted:

"Stop the terrible deed! Great Zeus does not want human sacrifice. At this very time, high on Olympus, he is planning how to save your son."

"Would your words were true," the king cried in anguish, "but you know the order of the oracle. What can I do?"

"Wait," said Heracles. "Wait with this deed of horror. Wait until the sun travels on its course toward the middle of the day. I know there will be a sign from heaven to prevent it."

Even while he was speaking, the gods were at work to save Phryxus. They used their godly power and they used their magic spells, and soon they created a ram, the like of which had never been seen before—a ram with a fleece of golden-spun hair shining bright as the sun during the midday hour. It was fleet as a deer and could fly as well as run. It could speak and understand speech!

The gods cried an order to the ram: "Go down to the mountain where you will see King Athamas and his people ready to sacrifice Phryxus. Put the boy on your back and take him where he will be safe from Ino and her persecutions. Do it speedily."

Swift as an eagle, the ram with the golden fleece flew from Mount Olympus to where King Athamas, surrounded by his people, stood ready for the sacrifice.

When the king and queen and Ino and the people saw the wondrous ram, they lost their power of speech and their eyes were blinded by the gleam of its golden fleece.

"Climb swiftly on my back," the ram cried to Phryxus. He did so at once. Then Helle spoke:

"Brother, you cannot leave me here to be destroyed by Ino's vengeance."

"Climb up behind me," Phryxus cried, and she did.

No sooner did the ram feel the weight of the two, than up it rose toward heaven, flying swiftly over mountains, over valleys, over streams. Phryxus and Helle thought it the most wonderful adventure they had ever had.

But after a time Helle became tired holding on to the ram's fleece. "Brother! My hands ache and I am tired. I cannot hold on much longer."

"You must hold fast, sister. We are at a great height and to fall off would be fatal to you. You must hold on with all your strength, Helle!"

Helle did the best she could. She held tight to the golden fleece as the ram flew over mountains and valleys. But her hands and arms grew more and more tired.

When they reached the watery strait dividing Europe from Asia, she could hold on no longer. The golden hair slipped through her fingers and she fell down, down, into the deep water! Ever since, the Greeks have called that water the Hellespont.

But the ram kept on flying until it reached Colchis, at the eastern shore of the Black Sea, where King Aeetes ruled.

All the city and the king rushed out at the sight of the ram with the golden fleece and the youth on it coming to the shore.

"From where have you come on this divine golden ram, good youth?" cried the king.

"I am Phryxus, son of Athamas, king of Thessaly. The gods sent me this divine golden ram to save me from being sacrificed."

"You will not be sacrificed here, good youth. You are most welcome. Stay with me in my palace, and I will treat you as if you were my own son."

And so Phryxus remained and was treated like a prince and beloved by all.

In thankfulness to the gods and the king, Phryxus sacrificed the ram to the gods and gave its golden fleece to King Aeetes.

The king was overjoyed at the wondrous gift, for nowhere in the land was there a fleece spun of gold and gleaming like the setting sun. He hung it in a sacred grove where the winds played softly and sweetly like divine flutes, and a dragon who never slept was put there as a guard.

There the golden fleece shone, brightening all the land like the sun traveling in its golden chariot.

There it shone until Jason came with many heroes and brought the golden fleece back to Thessaly, from whence the ram had begun its flight.

But the tale does not end here. The Greeks and the Romans of old and all weavers of myths and legends say the ram of the golden fleece went high, high up into the heaven, ever gleaming as it did in Thessaly. And in the heavens it is the Ram of the zodiac constellation.

TAURUS
THE BULL

Taurus the Bull was a very important creature in the zodiac and a god in the ancient world.

In the circle of the zodiac, Taurus consists of two main groups or clusters of stars: the Hyades and the Pleiades. Two very bright stars above these clusters are supposed to be the horns. The head is lowered down, shaped a little like a V, and is made up of five stars. One (the eye) is the great reddish-gold star named Aldebaran.

In the realm of the zodiac, Taurus the Bull was as important to the ancients as Aries the Ram, for, like Aries, Taurus at one time was connected with spring, the time of warmth and growth on the earth. But strangely enough at that time these stars were also thought to be connected with . . . death.

But this was so about two thousand years before the vernal equinox was in Aries. (The vernal equinox is a point on the equator occupied by the sun when spring begins.)

I told you earlier that when the sun entered the sign of Aries about three thousand years ago, the days grew longer than the nights and warmer, with a happy promise of life. (You must always try to keep in mind that the sun and the stars change their positions gradually as seen from the earth so that at the end of every two thousand years the sun appears in a different sign of the zodiac when spring begins.) Some two thousand years before the sun rose with the zodiacal sign of Aries each morning, it rose at springtime with the zodiacal sign of Taurus the Bull. Thus spring, for which mankind longed, was then under the stars in Taurus, bringing with it its many blessings. Taurus, therefore, was considered a most important constellation to mankind.

As a matter of fact, the worship of the bull had existed for thousands and thousands of years before the spring sun was in Taurus—particularly in Egypt. There he was the most important of the gods, for he was supposed to be a personification of Osiris, the foremost of Egyptian deities. High and low venerated the bull under the name of Apis, and great temples were built to him. Memphis was a holy city in which the sacred bull was kept. People came there from all the land to pay homage and bring offerings to the sacred animal. His birthday was set by the priests and was a time of special celebration. The death of such bulls was a period of much sorrow, and special burial places were built for the sacred animals. These places can be seen today and are a marvelous sight.

The bull was worshiped in other lands in a like way. In Sumeria, a division of Babylonia—the exact location of which is unknown—a bull with gigantic horns opened the new year and brought spring to life. The Cretans worshiped a sacred bull and told famous tales connected with this animal. The Chaldeans believed in the deity of the bull, and even the ancient Israelites had the golden calf, which was said to be an echo of bull-worship. The winged bull of the Assyrians was a god, and the Greeks tell how Zeus, their most important god, once changed himself into a bull.

In the zodiac, Taurus then coincided with the spring equinox (the time when day and night are the same length). It was the beginning of the new year!

The bull was also celebrated in all the arts. Winged bulls are found in most of the ancient temples and palaces in Eastern lands. Coins, gems, and embroideries were decorated with the sacred creature.

How and why this worship began we do not know. We can only guess from what we see in ancient stone carvings and tablets.

Perhaps star worship was the first worship of mankind, and the stars that looked like a bull to the ancients must have been part of that worship.

To those who believed in astrology, to be born under Taurus (that is, from April 21 to May 21 at the present time) signified having an attraction to power, great developing ability, and the capacity to resist troubles and difficult situations.

Strength and fearlessness are said to be the important points of those born at this time, which will lead them to unlimited success.

They are people said to have keen minds, to be joyous and lighthearted, and with strength of concentration. A great love for the arts will bring them happy days.

On the negative side, they are believed to be subject to strong likes and dislikes and violent tempers.

Women born under the sign of Taurus are considered devout and clinging, ready to do anything for the one they love.

Agate is the stone of this sign, the jonquil its flower.

THE HYADES

In the head of Taurus the Bull, in the circle of the zodiac, there are five stars that have been linked together throughout the world with soft gray skies, shadowy vapors, and rain. Not cold whipping rains, but life-giving spring rains sinking deep into the earth to awaken seeds to grow that bring food to man. These stars are called the Hyades. One of them, the most brilliant in all of Taurus and very brilliant among all the stars, is named Aldebaran. It is of such gleaming luster that the Babylonians called it the star of stars. It is this star that is said to be one of the eyes of Taurus.

There are many beautiful tales told about these five stars in every part of the world where men observed and studied them. Now I will tell you two of these stories. The first is an ancient Greek tale.

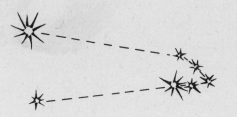

Tears of Grace
and Blessing

Years and years ago, when nymphs, those beings who disported themselves in woods and streams, roamed the land of Greece, there were among them five sisters. These five sisters had one brother, named Hyas, who was much beloved by them. Most of the time the sisters were together rambling in the cool green and in the fresh, running streams.

But often their brother Hyas was away hunting, and this grieved the sisters and made them unhappy.

"Why can't he always be with us?"

"Hunting is dangerous and there are many ferocious animals!"

"Some harm may come to him when he runs through the woods with his spear and bow."

Those words were always on the lips of the five sisters. But all their pleading with Hyas was of little use. He loved hunting passionately, and nothing could stop him from roaming with spear and arrows for stag and boar.

One time he was hunting wild boars in far Libya. They were ferocious animals, fierce of temper and dangerous. It required great courage and strength to attack them. But young Hyas was fearless and full of youthful daring.

One day he was following one of those long-snouted, bristly creatures, his sharp spear raised high. He and his companions had come into a dark wood of giant oaks hiding the sun, and there the boar turned on Hyas. Unafraid, Hyas threw the spear with all his strength, but it just grazed the beast's ear. Hyas's foot slipped on the green moss from the force of the throw, and he fell to the ground.

The wild, gray, angry animal attacked him fiercely and soon had done unto the handsome youth what the youth had wanted to do to him.

Birds and trees and all living creatures in the green world were saddened by the bloody sight of the dead youth!

But saddest of all were the five sisters.

"Hyas, our beloved brother, where art thou?"

"Our brother is dead!"

"We will never see him again."

"Why was he always hunting when we pleaded with him to stay with us?"

"Evil spirits led him to his death."

"Life is not worth living without him."

"Life is all black without him."

So they kept on crying and lamenting loudly and wildly, and the sound was heard from one end of the land to the other. It even reached up to the very heavens, and the gods high on Olympus heard it too.

Zeus, the mightiest of the gods, felt sorry for the five bereaved maidens.

"I grieve for those five unhappy sisters; their tears for their lost brother are without end. I will therefore turn them into stars and set them in heaven. There their tears of love and sorrow will turn into tears of grace and blessing for the earth and man."

And so Zeus raised the five nymph sisters to heaven, where they are the five stars in the face of Taurus and are called the Hyades.

There the five sisters still mourn and weep for their lost brother. Their soft warm tears turn into rain and come down to the earth, bringing life to the seeds underground that become food for man.

The Rain God on
the White Cloud

There is not a land where the Hyades, those five stars that make up the face of Taurus the Bull in the zodiacal circle, are not celebrated in great tales. Here is one they tell in China.

In that land it is said that Yu-Shih (or Ch'ih Sung Tsu) sits enthroned high up in the Hyades, which give life-bringing rain to the waiting earth.

One time, thousands of years ago, there was a terrible drought in China, during the reign of the emperor Shen Nung. The earth was parched and the dust feet-deep. In the rivers were only sand and stones, and both man and beast suffered. Prayers by the emperor and priests and people did not bring the good rain to the thirsty earth. The whole land was in a sad plight.

One day a wandering priest came to that stricken land, and the people saw by his clothes he was a holy man who prays for rain. At once there was great excitement.

"A holy pilgrim has come to our city who can bring rain with his prayers!" men and women shouted. "Let us run to the palace and tell this to the emperor."

They rushed pell-mell up to the palace gates, where stood the guards and the courtiers.

"There has come to the city a rain-praying pilgrim! Quick, tell the emperor!"

The courtiers ran to the emperor and told him the exciting news: "Oh, Heaven-born! There has come to our stricken city a holy man who might bring the rain we need so much!"

"Where is he? Where is he?" cried the emperor, rushing out among the people.

"In the marketplace!"

The emperor, the courtiers, and the people ran to the marketplace, where the pilgrim stood quietly and serenely.

"Holy pilgrim," spoke the emperor, "the people say your prayers bring rain. Help us! Our land is laid waste, and man and animal suffer sadly. The earth is dry as bleached bone and empty of the green growths we need for life. Help us in this terrible hour."

"What you ask of me, O Emperor," answered the priest, "is very simple and easily done. Get an earthen bowl, pour water into it, and bring it to me."

Quickly the priest's request was carried out. The

bowl, filled with water, was brought to him. The priest took it in his right hand, and with the left he plucked a branch from a tree on the nearby mountain. Then he raised the bowl high above his head, dipped the branch into the water of the bowl, and sprinkled it over the earth around him.

No sooner had he done this than, lo and behold!, the heavens grew dark and clouds gathered with the speed of running horses. The rain began to pour down in great torrents.

"A miracle!"

"Thank you, Holy pilgrim."

"The gods listened to your prayers!"

Old and young, rich and poor, high-born and low —all were shouting with joy.

The earth was happy, too, drinking the good, rich rain coming down without end. The rivers began swelling with the life-giving rain. And the animals in field, wood, and dale and the birds in the air were also drinking the sweet water.

The people kept on shouting their thanks and praises. But suddenly they stopped, for before their eyes something miraculous took place. There, in front of the emperor, his court, and all the people, the priest changed! He rose high in the air, still holding the bowl and branch in his hand; a white cloud was under his feet. His outer garments turned into yellow scale armor. On his head there was now a blue hat with a yellow band around it. Thus he stood on a white cloud before all, his watering bowl in his hand.

"He is one of the gods!" came loud from all throats. "He is a god from heaven who came to help us!"

Yu-Shih (or Ch'ih Sung Tsu) rose higher until he reached the five gleaming stars, the Hyades, and there he rested and has been resting ever since.

But on the earth, the emperor, the courtiers, and all the people recognized him as a god, the master and giver of rich rain: Yu-Shih (or Ch'ih Sung Tsu).

Ever since then, people in China have honored him as one of the gods, sitting on high among the five stars, the Hyades, that bring their land rich rain for life and food.

THE PLEIADES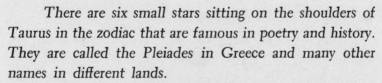

There are six small stars sitting on the shoulders of Taurus in the zodiac that are famous in poetry and history. They are called the Pleiades in Greece and many other names in different lands.

They are winter stars, and you can see them best on cold, clear nights. Sometimes when the night is glinting-sharp, you can see a seventh star, the lost star, and that one is also famous in poetry and stories.

These six or seven stars have had a very important meaning for thousands of years, for, as we have said, Taurus has been connected with birth and death! The time when the stars reach their height—midnight—is held sacred to the dead. Halloween brings memories of the ancient rites and customs observed at that time of the year. They are found in one form or another all over the world.

Since these stars also appear a few hours after midnight in the summertime when fruits and grain are ripening, they have a double meaning. Each area has its own series of tales. Here is one told in Polynesia by the Maori people.

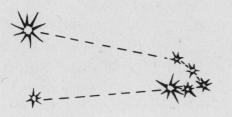

Little Eyes

When the Pleiades, those six (or seven) little stars sitting on the hump of Taurus the Bull, come to Polynesia, to the Maori tribes, there are great feasts and much singing and dancing, for it is then the beginning of the new year. Some of the Islanders called these stars the Seven Sisters, and others said they were the left eyes of seven great warriors.

In the very, very old days when the gods made the world, these little stars were one great glorious star, the Great Gleaming One. He shone more brilliantly than all other stars, with such radiant glory that all the earth was happy in its grand nightly beauty.

Of all those waiting for that star to shine, none waited more eagerly than Little Lake up among the hills.

When the magnificent star came out and bathed its reflection deep in Little Lake, the waves shimmered and rolled in bright joy.

But there was none of this joy in heaven about the great star. The other stars living in the robe of the sky were dimmed when that one star came forth. And that one star was very proud that he was brilliant enough to dim all the others. "I can outshine all the stars in heaven," the Great Gleaming One shouted loudly through the world.

Now Tane, creator of the world, the great god of water, woods, birds, and insects, heard this. It was he who had put all the stars in the vast basket of the Milky Way and had scattered them in the blue robe of the sky, and he wanted all to shine alike.

"I brought the stars into the world and they all have the same right to shine. I vow to punish this boaster for speaking such words."

Little Lake, that loved the Great Gleaming One, heard this and was frightened. It cried to Rangi, the sky father: "O Rangi, Sky Father who sees all, help me! I beg a favor of you! Tell the Great Gleaming One, my love, that great Tane said he will punish him for saying he can outshine all the stars of heaven."

"I cannot do anything against Tane, the creator of all," said Rangi.

Little Lake was unhappy, but the sun shone strong until Little Lake was only a mist. The wind took Little-Lake-Mist on its back and carried it high, high up over the mountains until it reached the Great Gleaming One, and then Little-Lake-Mist told him of Tane's anger and vow.

Tane gathered some of the powerful Shining Stars and they went with him to attack the Great Gleaming One. But he was ready. He saw them coming from afar, and he fled speedily to escape. Tane and the Shining Stars sped swiftly after him. The race went wildly through the sky, as Tane and those with him gained slowly on the Great Gleaming One.

Tane was getting impatient, so he picked up Aldebaran, the giant star, from Rangi's folds, and flung him with all his godly power at the Great Gleaming One, and . . . the boasting Great Gleaming One broke into pieces. Tane picked up the pieces and flung them away, with the mist of Little Lake around them. Where he threw them, they have stayed ever since—in the middle of Taurus. The Polynesian people call them the Matariki, "Little Eyes." We call them the Pleiades.

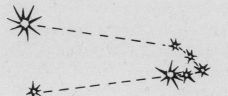

The "Mass"
in the Sky

In the ancient, ancient days there lived in the land of the Mayas, in Mexico, twin brothers called Hunapu and Xbalangue. They played the flute, they sang songs, and they practiced on the blowpipe for games and war.

They had many great adventures, but none so memorable as their strife with Zipacna, son of Vacub Kakix, the worst braggart in all the land of Mexico. He even bragged that he was sun and moon on the days when there was no sun and moon.

He also said he had made the earth and man on it and many other such bluffjammers. He was a very strong person—a great giant—and so powerful that he played ball with tall mountains.

Hunapu and Xbalangue decided to put an end to his silly boasting and bragging.

"Only children learning their first words would do such silly bragging," said Hunapu to Xbalangue.

"You are speaking pure words, brother. Even the winds laugh at that gibbering blown-up bag."

"We can stop him," said Hunapu, "and clear the air of him and his boasting."

"How?"

"Brother, let us call all our friends together. We can trust them, for no one likes big Zipacna, and with all heads together we will find a way."

They called their young friends from far and near, speeding the word that they needed help. Soon there were nearly four hundred of their friends—young, big, and strong. When the twin brothers Hunapu and Xbalangue told them why they had been asked to come, there was a great shout of agreement, for they all had had enough of Zipacna's boasting and bragging.

All kinds of schemes were put forward. In the end, Hunapu spoke: "Let us dig a deep hole for a house and begin to put up the house. Then we must find a way to get Zipacna into the hole and bury him under the beams."

Everyone agreed this was the best idea, and they went to work at once. Some of the young men went into the woods and cut great trees, while others, with the help of Hunapu and Xbalangue, began digging a deep hole for the foundation.

Zipacna was bathing in the river when he saw the youths dragging the giant trees.

"What will you do with the great trees you are dragging?" the giant asked.

"We need them for a house and we are dragging them to the hole our friends are digging."

"I will help you," Zipacna said, and he picked up the trees and put them on his shoulders so that the others did not have to drag them. They came to the place where the others were digging the hole.

"Why don't you stay with us and help us?" one of the young men said.

"That I will," answered Zipacna.

He stayed with them, and soon he learned they were plotting against him. But he made believe he did not know this, and began planning his revenge.

The hole was growing deeper every day.

"We have dug the hole as deep as we can," said Hunapu. "You are strong, Zipacna. Why don't you go down and help us dig deeper?"

Zipacna smiled and went down into the hole. After he was there for a time, he shouted up: "I am digging deeper!" But, instead, he was digging a hole next to the one for the house, where he would be safe when they tried to bury him in the deep hole.

"Ha," those above said, "now let us throw down rocks and the trees crosswise over him and then build the house on it. That way the braggart can never come out."

And they did this.

But Zipacna heard the words and laughed, digging away at the hole on the side for a shelter for himself. Soon it was big enough, and those above began throwing rocks and the big trees into the hole under the house. Zipacna stood on the side and was not hurt, but he cried out as if hurt, to fool those above.

Then they began to work hard building the house, and soon it was done.

"Now let us have a great celebration to honor our new house and a feast for the death of that giant braggart," they shouted.

Zipacna heard this and laughed. The youths and the two brothers Hunapu and Xbalangue went inside, to drink and sing and play and dance. That was just what Zipacna was waiting for.

For a time he let them dance and drink. Then he crawled under the foundation of the house. Slowly he put his giant shoulders, wider than a mountain, under the foundation. Next he put his great heavy hands on the ground and then suddenly gave a tremendous shove! That shove was so terrific that the house and everyone in it flew up high, high to the very sky, and there they became the cluster of stars the Mayan people call just "mass" to this very day—the cluster we call the Pleiades.

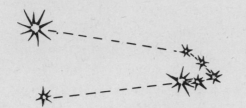

The
Dancing Ones

A band of Onondaga Indians was traveling along looking for good hunting grounds. Their chief, Ha-Ya-No ("Tracks-in-the-water"), was in front, warriors and women and children following.

They went through deep, dark forests and green waving ferns; they went through seas of green prairies. They went over hills and through rivers under the warm sun. They traveled easily for days. On the way they found game, fish, and berries.

Sometimes they traveled when the stars came into the sky and when the moon followed them.

So they came to Kan-ya-ti-yo, which in Onondaga language means "beautiful lake." It was a large lake full of swarming fish. Big fat game came to drink there and to bathe. And the woods were full of small and large animals.

The chief halted his tribe. "Here is good land, and the lake is full of fish. Deer and other game come here to drink. Over the hills are valleys filled with oak, beech, and chestnut and plenty of game and berries. It is a good place for us to camp. Here we will build our lodges for the winter. Let us thank the Spirit, who has been good to us on our way and is good to us now, giving us enough to eat and health and peace."

They built their lodges, hunted and fished and picked berries. There was enough for all to eat, and there was peace.

The Onondaga children had little to do, and the hours were moons long.

"Our fathers and uncles are hunting and fishing. Our mothers are busy in the fields and lodges. We have nothing to do."

"Let us play hunting," said the boys.

"We have no bows and arrows."

"Let us run after deer and look at the fish in the stream."

"We cannot follow the swift deer, and the fish are too quick for us to watch."

"Let us dance as our fathers and mothers do."

Everyone thought this was a good idea. So they found a large clear grassy place not far from the camp, and there they danced in their own way, as their fathers and mothers danced. They had a fine time together.

"Let us come here tomorrow and every day for our dance," they said.

So they went to dance the next day and the next, and they all liked it.

One day an old man came to where they were dancing. They had never seen such a man and were a little frightened. He was dressed in white feathers, and his hair shone like silver in the sun.

"Children of the Onondaga tribe, you must stop this dancing or evil will fall on you." The children only laughed and kept on dancing.

"We are not afraid," they shouted.

Day after day the man in white came to warn them,

and they always laughed at him and kept up their dancing.

One day the youngest of the children said: "It would be more fun if we had something to eat when we are tired."

"That would be nice," said another. "Why don't we ask our mothers for venison?" They all agreed.

The next day before going to their dance, the children asked their mothers for venison.

"Food gets lost on the way," said one of the mothers. "If you are hungry, you can come home to eat," said

another. "Why don't you pick berries and eat?" Each mother said something like this, and none gave the children anything.

So they went dancing without anything to eat. Each day they danced longer and longer, they liked it so much. The old man came now and then to warn them that evil would come of it, but they just laughed.

One day they danced much longer than usual because they felt very, very light. Then a funny thing happened! Suddenly they felt themselves floating in the air, high off the ground. They did not know why, but they just felt nice and light.

One of the boys shouted: "This is even nicer than dancing on the grass. Don't let us look back."

A woman saw the children floating high in the air and cried: "Come down! Come back!" But they kept on rising slowly.

She ran to the camp, shouting, shouting loud what she had seen. Then the women cried: "Let us give them food for which they had asked. That will bring them back."

Everyone got food and rushed out to where the children were slowly rising.

"Come back! Come back! Here are good things to eat. Please come back!" they shouted and begged.

"Come down and you can have anything you want. Only come down."

But the begging and crying did no good. The children were rising higher and higher. . . . Only one turned back to look at the crying women.

The children reached the sky and became the stars we now call the Pleiades. The Onondagas call them Oot-Kwa-Tah. The child that looked back became a falling star.

And the Pleiades twinkling and glimmering in the sky look as if they were dancing the dance of the Onondaga children.

GEMINI
THE TWINS

High up in the sky there are two big brilliant stars shining near each other in eternal friendship. They are probably the only two great stars in the zodiac so close together. In the circle of the zodiac they are Gemini the Twins, well known also as Castor and Pollux, or the Dioscuri, famous in ancient wars and legends.

If you spend a long time looking at these bright stars,

you will make out two figures. The two stars shining so brilliantly lie a distance east of Taurus and are the heads of the Twins. Two lines of light stars downward make the bodies, and there are clusters of stars showing the feet lying in the region of the Milky Way.

Through the ages these two brilliant stars have been the world's example of brotherhood and loving friendship, even as the idea of twins has been universal from the most ancient days. Many other meanings have been given to these two luminaries. Some held that they were the great healers of man. Others believed they were the bringers of warmth and food. But, whatever the belief, it was always associated with the idea of the universal "two": twins. This idea of "two"—twins—is found in endless examples throughout the world.

The double is repeated continuously in events and conditions in the universe. There are day and night, summer and winter, hot and cold, and so on without end. Castor and Pollux are the classic example of this worldwide order. In different lands they are named differently, but always with the same underlying principle of brotherly friendship.

The concept of such twin-meanings probably dates back to the times of the Babylonians and people of India, who told tales of twin horses riding high in the heavens. Then, when these peoples began spreading through the world and some became known as Greeks and others as Romans, they brought the ancient tales with them, changing them often according to the lands and the peoples who told them. And because of the spreading of Greek and

Roman mythology throughout the world, Castor and Pollux became the best-known of the twins.

They undertook every adventure together. As citizens of Sparta in Greece they were the pride of their countrymen. Castor was famous as a tamer of horses and as a fearless soldier; Pollux (also known under the name of Polydeuces) was the most famous boxer in the land. They were truly men without fear, ever ready to help those who fought with equal bravery.

In astrology it is said that those born under Gemini, May 22 to June 21, have a well-balanced dual personality, are well formed and have clear eyes. They are considered very sympathetic and helpful to their friends.

But like all human beings, Geminis also have their faults. They are said to be quick-tempered, and that often makes them unreliable and unreasonable.

Astrologists say women born under Gemini lack patience but are fine homemakers and love all things of beauty. They are also believed to be impulsive and affectionate and very generous.

Gemini is said to govern the health and strength of the arms and shoulders. Astrologically, the color of that zodiacal constellation is chestnut. Their gem is the beryl, and the flower is the trailing arbutus.

And now to the best-known tale of these two famous brothers.

Eternal Friendship

Castor and Pollux were twin brothers, but the tale also tells that Castor was mortal and could die, like all people, and Pollux was immortal and would live forever, like the gods high on Mount Olympus.

The brothers were always together and wore the same clothes, beautiful white armor, and they both rode magnificent white horses. Both were renowned as great warriors.

At the same time there lived another pair of twins named Idas and Lynceus, who were also famous for their strength and daring. There was much rivalry between these two pairs of twins and sometimes open warfare.

Idas and Lynceus had been courting two beautiful

maidens, Phoebe and Hilaetra. Castor and Pollux also tried
to win them. After a time the two young women decided
in favor of Idas and Lynceus, though they had been more
friendly with Castor and Pollux.

In those days women were often won by strength
and force. Castor and Pollux were angry; so once when
Idas and Lynceus were off on a hunt, the losers carried off
the maidens as their own.

When Idas and Lynceus returned and found their
brides gone, their anger was fiercer than a storm, but
they could do nothing against Castor and Pollux, who had
greater power at the time. But from then on the rivalry
and the bitter anger between the two pairs of twins grew
worse.

A war broke out against Sparta, and Idas and
Lynceus were on the side against Castor and Pollux.
The two pairs of twins met in violent combat, and Lynceus
mortally wounded Castor, who fell off his white steed.

Pollux leaped from his horse and took his wounded
brother into his arms.

"My end has come," whispered Castor, breathing
hard. "Farewell, brother!" His head fell and he breathed
no more.

"Castor! Castor! Brother!" cried Pollux. But no sound
or motion came from Castor.

Then Pollux knew his brother was no more among
the living. In burning rage he leaped on his horse and,
seeing Lynceus not far off, rode at him in wild fury.

"I've come to avenge my brother," Pollux roared,
attacking Lynceus.

"I'll send you where Castor is," screamed Lynceus, hitting back with all his might. The combat was short, and soon Lynceus was on the ground. The battle was over; victory was on Pollux's side.

"My brother is avenged," cried Pollux, "but it will not bring him to life. Gods on Olympus, my brother is dead! Zeus! Father! Castor is dead! Do you hear me?"

Friends came to the hero and tried to ease his sorrow. But it was of no use.

"Castor is dead! My brother is dead!" he kept on crying. "I don't want to live without him."

Spoke one of his friends: "Come, Pollux, it is one of our honored customs to set up a trophy at our gymnasium to show a brother's death has been avenged."

With lowered head Pollux rode to the gymnasium, followed by his friends, and there, on a long painted pole, he placed Lynceus's sword to commemorate the victory on the battlefield.

But that did not ease Pollux's sorrow. He shouted to the heavens: "I do not want to live on earth without Castor. I want to die."

The gods on Olympus heard the unending lamentation. Zeus spoke to his messenger: "Go to Sparta and bring the grieving Pollux to our dwelling."

The messenger came to Pollux: "I have been sent to take you to Olympus. You want to die but you cannot die. You are the son of Zeus and you are immortal."

Soon Pollux was among the gods on Mount Olympus before his father, great Zeus.

"You can now stay among us forever," said Zeus.

"Father Zeus," said Pollux, "I do not want to be among the ever-living gods unless my brother Castor is here with me. I cannot live without him."

"Son," Zeus answered, "I cannot bring Castor here among the immortals, but, seeing how much you love him, I will grant you a part of your wish. All your days you can be one day under the earth with Castor, and the next day he can be with you up here. Thus you will be able to be with him all the time."

Pollux thanked his father over and over again. "I am satisfied with your decision as long as I can be with Castor."

"Since you are so devoted to your brother Castor and he to you, I will also set your images as great stars among the stars of heaven, so you will be forever an example of eternal friendship and love."

Thus Zeus set the two great shining stars in the heavens, close to each other as the Gemini, the Twins eternal, symbol of brotherly friendship for all the world.

CANCER
THE CRAB

A certain small group of stars in the great heavens is often difficult to see, yet is important in the history of stars and lore and tales. I am speaking of Cancer the Crab in the zodiac, which lies not far from Gemini in the east.

The Chaldeans and later Plato called this constellation the "Gate-Man" through which the shadowy souls descended from heaven into the human body.

In different lands there are different names for these misty stars: the Lobster, the Beehive, the Manger, the Crayfish, the Little Cloud, the Little Mist. The Egyptians called them the Scarab, which is the sacred beetle that rolls the sun with its front claws in its daily voyage through the sky. The weather was also foretold by these stars.

There was one more important reason why this group of stars was of great significance to the ancient world: About three thousand years ago the sun, that divine blessing to man, reached it at the summer solstice (at the present time the sun is between Taurus and Gemini at the summer solstice).

Astrologers sometimes did not agree about the action of this group of stars. One great astrologer in the early days said that someday, in midsummer, under the stars of Cancer, there would come such terrible storms and wild sweeping rains that they would destroy the whole world. But other astrologers claimed that in Cancer there was the birth of our conscious soul; that these stars were the very egg, the very cradle, of the universe; that they were the symbol of the sea, the mother of all life. According to their beliefs, the lucky ones born under the sign of Cancer (June 22 to July 23) will have strong personalities, bring forth fine families, and create good homes. They will be successful from childhood up, having deep understanding and warm sympathy. They also encourage the expression of individuality and strive for developing character and success.

In their opinion, women born in the sign of Cancer are likely to be deeply interested in music and drama and the arts—literature, in particular. They have charm and are lively and pleasant. All in all, they are gay and happy and brilliant.

But sometimes, those who come under the influence of Cancer may expect violent death.

The gem of Cancer the Crab is the ruby, and its flower the water lily. Some astrologers say its color is silver; others, that the colors are green and russet.

There are as fine stories about these little stars as about the big stars, and now I will tell you one.

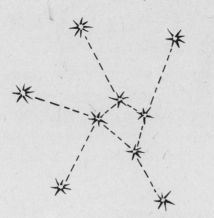

The Great Battle
of Heracles
and the Hydra

Who was Heracles, whom some called Hercules? Heracles, or Hercules, was perhaps the greatest hero of the Greeks. He fearlessly fought twelve fierce battles no mortal man could have fought.

Who was the Hydra? The Hydra was a terrible water monster living in the swamps of Lerna in Greece. It was a gruesome scourge in that beautiful, sacred countryside by the sea. All the people far and near were ravaged by the monster, and no traveler who went through the country in which the Hydra dwelled came out alive. It had the hairy body of a giant dog, and on its shoulders it had snaky heads—some said nine, some fifty or a hundred or a thousand. All these snake heads were mortal except one, which was encased in gold; that one was immortal. The sheer sight of the beast brought death, and the very breath of the monster was so poisonous that it killed those who inhaled it.

All the land knew of this terror, and many a brave man had tried to destroy it—and had paid with his life.

Now, in those days Heracles, in a moment of madness, had committed a grave wrong, and the gods ordered him to atone for it by going to King Eurystheus and doing whatsoever he ordered him to do.

Heracles went to the king and stood before him with bowed head. "O great King," he said, "I committed a tragic crime in moments of madness, and the gods have ordered me to come to you and do whatever task you give me."

"I know what you have done, great Heracles," said the king, "and you must atone for it."

Heracles stood, eyes lowered, and did not answer.

"You are known," continued the king, "as the bravest and strongest man in the land. I will give you twelve tasks to do that no man has ever been able to perform before."

"I will do whatever you order."

First the king ordered Heracles to slay the Nemean lion, the giant beast whose skin could not be pierced by iron, stone, or bronze.

Heracles fought and finished off the beast.

Then the king ordered him to destroy the Hydra,

the water monster that had its lair in Lerna, where it was a curse to the land and people. Heracles set out in his chariot with his faithful friend and charioteer Iolus to obey the order of the king. Soon they came to Lerna by the sea, not far from the city of Argos.

They had reached a grove near the place where the Hydra had its lair. Heracles halted the horses and his chariot under an old willow with long branches thick with slender leaves.

"Here I leave the chariot with you, Iolus," said Heracles. "You watch the steeds. I will also leave my sword with you. I think my good club and arrows will be enough to end the monster."

He put down his sword and stepped from the chariot, carrying only the club and arrows. Thus armed, he went into the tangled growth of the grove.

The gods on high Olympus were greatly concerned with the deeds of Heracles. Some were on his side, ready to help him; some were against him, trying to hinder him. The goddess Athena was on the hero's side and pointed out to him a plane tree, near the mouth of a river, under which he would find the monster. She also told him that burning arrows would drive the monster out of his lair.

Heracles entered the thick tangled grove slowly and began shooting flaming arrows under the plane tree. No sooner had he begun than the monster raced out at him. Heracles held his breath so as not to inhale the poisoned air, caught hold of the beast, and began beating off the snake heads with his club. But no sooner was a head off, than three new ones grew in its place. Besides, the beast had twined its body around Heracles and was trying to throw him down.

Heracles was battling with all his strength and never saw a giant crab sent by the goddess Hera, who was against him, crawling out of the nearby swamp, coming to help the Hydra. Slowly the crab crawled up to Heracles and bit him in the foot. Heracles felt the sting and crushed the shell of the crab with his heel, killing the creature and continuing the battle.

The contest was growing longer and fiercer. Then Heracles, in a voice nearly as strong as that of his father Zeus, roared out to Iolus standing with the chariot: "Iolus, bring my sword and some burning bushes to sear the places where I cut off the snake heads so they can't grow again."

Iolus rushed up, burning bushes in one hand and the sword in the other.

Heracles clubbed the snake heads off, and Iolus seared the places from which they had grown so no others could grow there.

But there was one head left, the immortal one. Heracles threw his club to the ground, took up his sword, and severed the immortal head encased in gold. The monster fell down quickly. Heracles picked up the hissing snake head and rushed to bury it under a heavy rock. Then he tore the dead monster apart and dipped his arrows into its gall. From then on, any wound, however small, inflicted by those arrows brought certain death.

But Hera felt sorry for the crab she had sent on the fatal errand to help the Hydra, and so, to reward it, she picked up the pieces, set them in the heavens, and turned them into stars. And there the crab, turned into stars, has remained and has become the zodiacal constellation known as Cancer the Crab.

LEO
THE LION

If you look long at the friendly blinking stars lying between Cancer and Virgo on a gentle spring night, you will gradually see five stars in a half circle like a sickle or a question mark. Below them is a great shining star that might be called the handle of the sickle.

This "end" star has been named Regulus and is very famous. Much has been told and written about it. Once

upon a time it was believed that Regulus ruled the affairs
of the stars. It was Regulus who, like a monarch, kept order
among the heavens' scintillating inhabitants. In Persia this
star was called "the Guardian of Heaven."

If you have a grand and lively imagination, the
"sickle" can be called the mane of . . . a lion. Look
farther back and you will see two stars set apart and, following the creation of your imagination, you may call them
the back of the lion. Then farther on, to the east, follow a
bunch of dancing stars that can be called the tail of the
king of the beasts. There is a fine story about this tail that
I will tell you later.

For thousands of years these stars were known as
Leo the Lion in all lands of the Near East and the West
as well. For Greeks and Romans, Persians and Babylonians,
they had a definite meaning. Some lands saw different animals in them: In China they were a horse; in South America
they were a puma leaping on its prey.

It was probably the Babylonians or the Egyptians
who first saw in those stars the form of a lion. And the lion
held an important place in their life, for the sun came into
that constellation at an important time of the year.

About five thousand years ago the Chaldeans first observed this phenomenon. They saw that the summer was
warmest and the sun strongest when the sun reached the constellation of Leo; it was the time of the summer solstice. As
I have explained, the relative position of the constellation
with respect to the equinoxes has changed since then, but
the belief is still the same as it was thousands of years ago.

The solstices are the points in the sky (twenty-three

and a half degrees above and below the equator) reached by the sun when it seems to stand still as it turns around in its annual journey north and south of the equator. It was to the ancients a most significant time of the year. And since they believed that the actions of the sun were regulated by the stars, these stars were prominent gods with strong influences on life.

Astrologers put forth great claims for those born between July 24 and August 23 under the stars of Leo the Lion, the ruler of the animal kingdom. These persons are said to have great pride and fiery spirit, nobility and courage, and love life and its joys. They are thought likely to have great charm and have a happy and jovial disposition, and because of this to make friends easily and be very popular.

With such personalities they retain their youth through many years, during which they are eager for amusement and friendship. But they are also very impulsive and hotheaded and must watch out for the pitfalls such qualities bring.

Women born under Leo are said to be warmhearted and sympathetic. They love their homes and enjoy domestic life. Truly, they have royal attributes representing protectiveness and love. Those born under the sign of Leo the Lion would become leaders in the world.

The gem of Leo is the sardonyx; the flower is the poppy; and the color is gold. The eagle is the symbol of Leo.

Some astrologers give different gems and flowers for these stars.

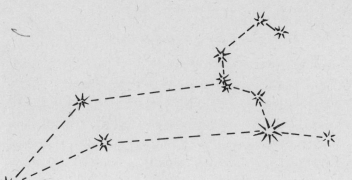

The Gleaming
Tail of
Leo the Lion

Alexander the Great of Greece conquered half the ancient world, part of which was Egypt. When this great warrior could no longer rule, one of his generals, a Macedonian, Ptolemy by name, took over the reign of the kingdom of the Nile, which is Egypt. He ruled so justly and so wisely that nobles, priests, and the people asked him to become their king. Thus the Macedonian dynasty of the Ptolemies began. There were sixteen of them throughout the years and all of them strove to make Egypt famous. At that time Memphis was the holy capital. Alexandria, with its magnificent marble tower in the harbor and the most famous library of ancient days, was one of the great cities of the time. Food, gold, spices, and pearls made up its daily commerce.

Many neighboring countries looked on Egypt jealously, and there were endless plots to conquer the throne. The Assyrians were enemies of Ptolemy III, and they had destroyed his sister, whereupon Ptolemy decided to attack them and avenge her death. He gathered his army and made ready to leave. But his wife Berenice, she of the famous spun-gold tresses, feared for her husband's safety and success.

She was talking to her favorite lady-in-waiting: "There is no end to wars. And war means death and destruction and maiming."

"It has always been thus, O beautiful Queen Berenice. Our tears and prayers to stop the men from fighting are of no help."

"I fear for my husband's life. Let us pray to the great goddess Aphrodite, who has looked upon me so kindly, and I will make a special precious offering to her if she brings my husband back to me safely. Send a maid to the priests of the goddess's temple saying that I want to come there for prayer and to make a special vow."

The temple was a great stone building surrounded by a ring of chambers. In front of it was the sacred lake and gardens with perfumed flowers. Early in the morning the chief priest broke the seal of the door to the sanctuary, closed the night before after the last prayer. Next he lighted the censors to perfume the chamber and brought warm water and washed the statue of Aphrodite. Then he put on it clothing and jewels, and ended by applying cosmetics to the face. This done, he embraced the statue and sang a hymn to the goddess.

From afar he heard the coming of Queen Berenice and her noble attendants. The queen, tall and very beautiful, her gold-spun hair hanging down her embroidered ocher tunic, entered the holy chamber and kneeled before the statue of the goddess Aphrodite.

"Divine Goddess," she prayed, "return by husband victorious and unharmed from the war against the Assyrians and I will give you the most beautiful and the most precious possession I have. I vow here that I will give you my golden tresses treasured by me, by my husband, and by all my people, if my husband returns unharmed and victorious." Then she arose from her knees and left, walking backward.

The priest undressed the holy statue, washed it, and perfumed the sanctuary. Then he closed the doors and sealed them.

Ptolemy went to the war and soon returned, victorious and unharmed. Great was the rejoicing and great were the festivities all over Egypt. King Ptolemy, Queen Berenice, and the statues of the gods were carried through the streets in a long procession and worshiped by thousands.

The next morning the queen and some attendants went to the temple of the goddess Aphrodite and into the sanctuary where the statue had been prepared. Berenice prostrated herself before it.

"Great Goddess Aphrodite, I give thanks to you for guarding my husband and helping him to a great victory.

I have come to carry out my vow." Then she said to one of the ladies, who held a pair of shears, "Cut off my tresses and give them to me."

The lady did as she was ordered, and Queen Berenice took the tresses and laid them on the altar.

"Here, O glorious goddess, I give you the part of me I most value and that I think most beautiful—my golden hair. This, for your divine help."

She and her ladies left, walking backward, and the priest performed the usual rites. Then he closed the doors of the sanctuary, sealing them as he always did.

All afternoon and through the night there were festivities and great rejoicing. The next morning the chief priest came as usual to the sanctuary to prepare the statue for worship. He lit the lamp and stopped as if petrified! The altar was empty!

The golden tresses Queen Berenice had brought to the goddess as an offering were gone! He rushed out, shouting hoarsely: "Arise! Help! A terrible sacrilege! A thief has stolen the golden hair of our queen. The golden tresses Queen Berenice gave to our great goddess are gone. Holy priests, come! Search! A terrible deed has been done!"

In a few moments the temple was in a turmoil. Priests ran in all directions shouting, looking, questioning.

Quickly King Ptolemy and Queen Berenice heard of the tragedy, the sacrilege!

Their anger was more black than a cloudy moonless night.

"It cannot be!" the queen screamed.

"Death! Death to the thief!" the king said grimly.

Both rushed to the sanctuary to see the horror with their own eyes. The altar was empty. A thief had stolen the queen's gleaming tresses.

Berenice wept and Ptolemy looked around slowly with hard-set eyes. Priest and courtiers stood silent. The ruler spoke to the priest: "The temple and the sanctuary are in your keeping. You are the guardian. You seal the doors. Only one of you could have stolen my queen's beautiful tresses. They must be returned by tonight or you will all pay for the crime with your lives. The queen and I will return this evening to the sanctuary, and the tresses must be on the altar where the queen laid them." Then the royal pair left.

A leaden silence fell on all. The king's words were law. All day long there was questioning and searching, and searching and questioning. The thief was not found, nor were the tresses. The fatal hour was approaching.

Evening came . . . no tresses and no thief!

King Ptolemy and Queen Berenice came to the temple with their nobles and attendants.

"My wife's tresses are not on the altar," the king said sternly.

There was a dull silence; only the stars in the sky moved in blinking light. Silence. The priests saw death in the eyes of the ruler.

Suddenly someone was speaking.

Among the attendants of the court was a Greek astronomer, Conon of Samos by name. He was honored and respected by all. In the frightening silence, he raised his voice. "Great ruler of the land of Egypt and beautiful Queen Berenice," he said, "your threatening anger and unhappiness are uncalled for. Your golden tresses, O Queen, are here for all to see. Look up high. Turn your eyes to the sky and look at the divine constellation of Leo the Lion. There at the end of his body is a wonderful gleaming cluster of stars. They are your golden tresses, Queen Berenice. The marvelous, gold-spun hair you vowed to the great goddess Aphrodite is too beautiful to be seen only by the few permitted to come to the temple's holy sanctuary. Such rare beauty should be seen by all the world. And so these tresses of our beautiful queen were taken by the goddess up to the heavens, to shine there forever for all the world to admire. No holy priest here took them."

He was silent and a load heavy as a pyramid was taken off the shoulders of all those present.

King Ptolemy and Queen Berenice were pleased and content, and so was all of Egypt and all the world. For ever since, everyone can have the joy of looking at the glorious cluster of stars, *Coma Berenice* (Hair of Berenice), that makes the tail of Leo the Lion in this constellation of the zodiac.

VIRGO
THE VIRGIN

When you look at the endless sky at night, and look long, long, you will see a line of stars, irregular and a little spread at the sides, with one far more brilliant than the others. Look longer and strain your imagination and little by little you, as many have done through the thousands of years before you, will begin to see the figure of a maid.

The very brilliant star is named Spica, and four stars are above it. More stars are higher up, more below, and there are stars on the sides. If you fill the space between these stars, you will see the figure of a maid in floating draperies, arms on the sides and wings extended, and there you have Virgo. The right hand is somewhat raised; in the left she holds a sheaf of wheat or corn—stars coming down from scintillating, brilliant Spica.

Virgo is surrounded on the northwest by the zodiacal constellation Leo, and the north by the Coma Berenice's stars about which I have just told you. Libra is to the east of her, and the stars of Corvus, Crater and Hydra are to the southwest. On the west are the stars of Leo again.

Among the Chinese this star Spica and another bright star named Arcturus almost due north were known as the Dragon's Horns. The Chinese reckoned the new year from the time the full moon was seen between these two stars. Spica was called by the Chinese "the Venerable God of Long Life," and named Shou Hsing.

Virgo the Virgin was probably first noted by the Sumerians or the Babylonians. There is perhaps no constellation in heaven better known the world over than Virgo. She appears everywhere in one form or another, under many names, for she is the symbol of Mother Earth, the goddess of fertility giving food to mankind.

Long, long ago she may have been Ishtar, the magnificent goddess of the Chaldeans. Her blazing adventures to rescue her husband from death are repeated in many versions of mythology throughout the world.

Strangely enough, Virgo—or Ishtar (Chaldean) or

Isis (Egypt) or Aphrodite (Greece), or the Corn Mother (the Americas)—is also connected with death! But isn't Mother Earth sleeping, dead, for half the year?

Astrology has much to say for those born between August 24 and September 23 under Virgo the Virgin, the only maiden constellation in the zodiac. Its name is feminine and a female child born in that month may be old-maidish, but she will be modest and quiet. She will be retiring and will like cooking and needlework. She will be a good mistress of the domestic arts and will accomplish them in an orderly manner. She will be the ideal of moral purity, chastity, and cleanliness.

In general, those born under Virgo are witty and of an ingenious mind. They love music and poetry and mathematics and the sciences. Their fundamental nature is graceful and charming, and they are discriminating in their taste. Though they are conservative, they have good reasoning and critical minds.

The stone for this sign is jasper, and the flower is the cornflower. The color varies: most say it is a beautiful deep blue; others say it is black speckled with blue.

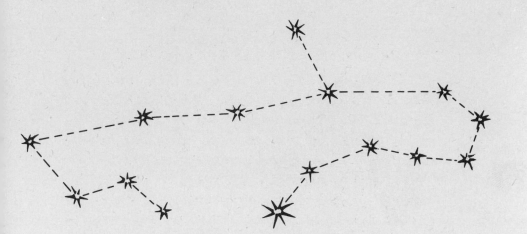

Isis and
the Starry Road
in Heaven

Glorious Virgo the Virgin in the zodiac was known in all lands of the world, for, as the Great Mother, she was the symbol of the earth.

In Egypt, Virgo was called Isis, and she carried in her hand the sacred ear of gleaming golden-tasseled corn. That was the symbol of her greatness, for it gave food to mankind. With that magic corn she created the wondrous path in heaven that has given joy to the world ever since. And this is how it happened.

Nut, the All-Mother goddess of Egypt, had five children. Three were boys and two were girls, and one of these was Isis. Isis was the most famous goddess of

Egypt, for she brought food, truth, and justice to the land.

One of the three sons was Osiris, "the Lord of Everything." Isis and her brother Osiris were married, as was the custom in Egypt in those days. There was also Horus, with the head of the falcon. He was the sky god, and the sun and the moon were his eyes. These three were close-knit in love and friendship and were called the Triad.

Then there was the third brother, Seth, but a brother only in name. He was a very ancient god known as "the son of Nut of great strength," and lord of the south. He was a god of the sky and thunder, beloved by soldiers for his fierce temper. But he was an evil god, wild and reckless and jealous of the Triad—Isis, Osiris, and Horus. He was always plotting against them and battling with them.

Sometimes there was open, fierce war between Seth

and Horus. Then there was raging commotion in the heavens. Horus fought with lightning as a spear, and Seth hurled arrows at him.

One day there was one of those terrible battles between these two.

> Seth sharpened his arrows in him;
> He shaketh the Earth and Sky with his thunderstorms;
> His magic powers are mighty conquering his enemy.*

Seth had seen Horus coming along in the sky, and he had decided to attack him.

"Now I will finish you and rid the sky of you."

Roaring fiercely, he flew at him.

But Horus had no fear and shouted loud: "Come on! Your words are a little wind in the morning. I will make an end of you who are an enemy and not a brother."

They began battling, Seth shooting his sharp, deadly arrows and Horus hurling his spears of lightning. The heavens were in wild turmoil.

Then Horus hurled his lightning spear with all the power he had, and it wounded Seth. The wound was painful, and he roared so loud and long, it sounded like never-ending thunder on the earth, and all Egypt was frightened.

"Roar, you deceitful, faithless creature they call my brother. Roar and learn that you have not the power to destroy me," cried Horus. And he flew off into the vast space.

* Translated by Max Muller.

Seth seethed with fury, but all he could do was wait for the wounds to heal. In time they did, but the hatred in him burned fiercer than ever.

"I will yet destroy these three with my strength and cunning. I'll bide my time. The three together are stronger than I am, but I can destroy them one at a time."

He watched and waited with wily silence for his chance. One day he saw Isis in the distance, alone in the sky.

"She is alone and I can capture her without fear. I will destroy her and bury her under the black raging waters so none will find her."

Swiftly he followed her, but she had seen him and ran fast. A wild race began between the two through the blue sky and the weaving clouds—Isis far ahead, for she was fleet of foot, and Seth, the Evil One, straining hard to get her.

Isis's hands were outstretched, in one of them the magic ear of corn, for she could run faster that way.

The winds blew wildly around her, and it was not easy, running with nothing solid under her feet. Suddenly the magic ear of corn, torn by the wind, broke open and the kernels began falling and spreading, falling and spreading, falling and spreading all around her under her feet. And as they fell they turned into stars and stardust. Isis now felt solid ground beneath her and so could run faster.

The race went on, with Seth falling farther behind while Isis was forging farther ahead.

Seth saw that he would not catch her.

"The next time she'll not escape," he said sullenly.

Isis realized that her ugly brother was not behind her and that she was safe. She looked back, at the vast road of dusty stars around the world that had come from the sacred grains, and she was happy. It has been a happy sight ever since, and has been called the Milky Way.

That is the tale they tell in Egypt about Isis—or Virgo—the sixth constellation in the zodiac in the heavens.

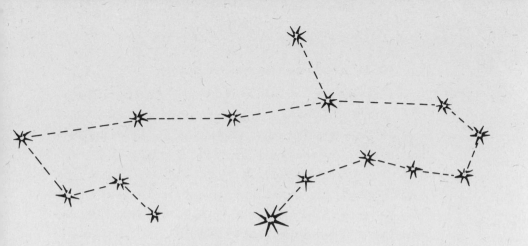

When the Last of the Gods Left Greece

Here is the tale about Virgo they
tell in Greece. There was a time, an eternity ago, when
the Greek gods lived among the people in the land of
Greece and took part in their daily life. There was happiness everywhere. That was in the golden age when King
Cronus ruled.

Life then was without sin, and there was peace
more beautiful than a rainbow. It was always spring, and
food grew in rich plenty for man to take. There was no
hard labor; when the gods walked among men, there was
only friendship and kindliness.

One goddess in particular liked to be in the midst

of the mortals. Her name was Astraea, goddess of innocence and purity, daughter of Themis, goddess of justice.
Astraea roamed the woods and the cities, filling them with
her heavenly blessings.

Then Zeus became the great god of Greece. He
looked around the world and thought there should be a
change in its order. "I think it would be better if the
world were divided into two seasons. It is too even now."

"How would you divide it?" asked one of the gods.

"One part would be balmy and warm and the other
sharp and cold so men would work harder and become
stronger."

"They may not like this."

But Zeus did what he said he would do. And the
golden age turned into the silver age. Just as one of the
gods had said, men were not satisfied with the turn of life.
They grumbled and complained: "It is not warm and we
must live in caves."

"We must work hard and for long hours."

"Sowing and reaping bring aches to our bodies."

The good goddess Astraea, who was always among
them, heard these complaints and tried to bring comfort.
"Even though life is not so simple," she said, "there are
still in your world peace and innocence."

"But when there is cold with cutting winds that
bring pain, we cannot think of virtues. We are too busy
in sweating hard labor for our daily food."

"Food for which you labored hard tastes sweeter.
Labor is a pleasure and it is also a pleasure to conquer
hard tasks."

But the pleading of the good goddess did not satisfy

man. Trouble began among them, and then came the brass age.

Men knew anger and discontent. They went hunting and destroying. Many of the gods no longer liked to be among men. They began leaving the land and going up to their heaven. But the goddess Astraea was faithful. She stayed with the Greeks, wishing and hoping they would once again be as they had been in the golden age.

"So long as there are innocence and purity," she said, "man will live a good life."

Men heard but did not heed. Ugly, vicious forces came into their lives. Suspicion! Hatred! Jealousy!

The iron age had come into the world.

The age of crime and war. Honor fell into the deepest abyss. Innocence and purity were only pale distant shadows. Men's minds were poisoned with hatred, and they fought brutal wars to conquer others.

The gods who were still among men saw this tragedy and fled to their heavenly home. Only Astraea still remained. She looked sadly at the Greek world, and there were tears in her eyes.

"All the gods are gone from the land and there is no place for me in this horror. They do not want me. All around me is tragic destruction. I must leave them too, but I will return to them if they give up their terrible ways."

She trembled and slowly rose into the endless space. She rose higher and higher until she reached the limitless stars. There she was called Virgo the Virgin, a crown of stars on her head and stars all about her.

Through the ages she has been shining up on high,

bright with innocence and purity. She is forever looking down on man, hoping to return when men will be as they were in the golden age. And then she again will be Astraea, the goddess of innocence and purity, and will bring happiness and joy to the world.

LIBRA
THE SCALES

Libra is the name given to a small cluster of stars lying between the zodiac constellations Scorpius and Virgo. Its history has been argued by many astronomers, some holding that it was part of Scorpius. The two brightest stars of Libra are still sometimes called the Northern and Southern Claws.

Some three thousand years ago, on the day the sun

rose in Aries and spring began, autumn came six months later, on the day that the sun rose in Libra. When this occurred, the day was equal in length to the night. Hence Libra occupied a special distinction in men's thoughts in those centuries.

In myth and history Libra thus was represented by the perfect balanced scale that had an important meaning in the ancient world:

It meant equally balanced justice among men—an important virtue in every part of the universe. And they noticed it also in the equally balanced arrangement in nature: day and night, the movements of the sun and moon, the movements of the sea.

So important did early man consider this equally balanced arrangement that they carried the scale into the very heaven and made it a part of the zodiac—the only non-living symbol in it.

The days of the equinoxes, which are March twenty-first and September twenty-third, are very important in the realm of religion. For when the sun in its yearly wanderings around the sky crosses the equator (which occurs twice a year, at the spring and autumn equinoxes), day and night are equally balanced in duration.

The ancient Israelites called the month of the autumnal equinox Tishri, and the first day of that month was and is still called Rosh Hashana, when the living and the dead were and are judged equally and their good and bad deeds were and are justly balanced.

No wonder the ancients took the scales as a religious symbol, on which souls, virtues, and evil acts were tried and balanced.

It is believed that the Babylonians were the first to use the scales as a symbol in the zodiac. Others say the Egyptians began it because it was the harvest time when the grain was weighed to assess the properly balanced amount of taxes. For the Chinese, Libra was a sign of justly balanced administration.

Some authorities claim the sign began with the Romans. It is said that before them, the little group of stars now known as Libra was the end of the claws of Scorpius. Even today two of the brightest stars of the group, as I said, are called the Northern Claw, and the other the Southern Claw. The separation from Scorpius is said to have taken place at the time of Julius Caesar, though this does not sound quite correct. That ancient dictator is often pictured holding scales as a sign of his great justice to all the world. But there are many carvings with the same symbol much before Julius Caesar. Often, on these records, kings held the scales to show their justly balanced rule. Then gradually the human figure was eliminated and only the scales were left.

There must have been an even division from the time the zodiac was arranged. There could not have been division into eleven; twelve always has been and still is a very important number in folklore and in calculation in the world, as I stated earlier.

The small group of stars named Libra—four of which are very bright—are to the right of and above Scorpius and stand where the autumnal equinox was a few thousand years ago. And it is normal to believe that Libra is as ancient as the time when star-students learned of the two days of the year when the hours are equally balanced between light and dark.

Astrologers have many good things to say about people born when Libra rules the sky. First, it is the seventh sign of the zodiac, and seven is considered an important number in life and lore. There are seven days in the week, and there are seven colors in the rainbow. There are seven sacred candlesticks, and there are many more sevens in life.

Venus is claimed as the goddess of Libra and the diamond its stone. The soft, lovely violet is the flower of the sign and water-green its color.

Astrologers give those born under Libra many good qualities. They say that men born from September 24 to October 23 are manly and fine human beings, pleasant-tempered and of good nature. They are believed to be just, upright, and properly balanced, like the star of their birth, and to like science, and be good students. They are also said to be generous and to like excitement.

Often they will have blue eyes and yellow or auburn hair. Since Libra is the sign of perfectly equal balance, those born at that time are said to have an equally balanced intellect and cultured mind.

Finally, astrologers claim that Libra, perfect balance, symbolizes the Sabbath of the Lord.

And now, here is a tale of Libra.

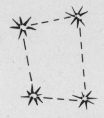

The King Who
Was Found Wanting
in the
Heavenly Balance

When Nebuchadnezzar, the great king of Babylon, conquered the Israelite city of Jerusalem, he took away the sacramental vessels from the holy temple. He commanded these to be brought to the house of his own gods, made of gold and silver, bronze and iron and wood and stone. He also ordered his officers to capture those Israelites of royal and noble descent who would be of value to his own kingdom.

"Seize their men," he commanded, "who are well favored and skillful in all wisdom and cunning and are rich in understanding. Bring into bondage such as have the knowledge of visions and dreams. They must be the kind who are fit for my kingly household."

So the officers took by force such as the king ordered, and among them was Daniel, who was renowned for his birth, his knowledge, and his wisdom.

The captured sacred vessels and the Israelite nobles were all brought to Shinar, where King Nebuchadnezzar held court and housed his own idols. There many marvelous happenings took place in the life of Daniel, and in each he proved that he was a man wise in thought and act and keen in the interpretation of dreams. All these adventures you will find in the Book of Daniel in the Bible.

Many a time Daniel pleaded with King Nebuchadnezzar to mend his ways and cease worshiping worthless idols. Often the king followed Daniel's words for a short time, but soon he would again fall into the sinful worship of his images. For this he was much punished by the Lord.

Then Nebuchadnezzar died, and his son Belshazzar came to the throne. He, like his father, turned his face from the true Lord and worshiped the idols. The Bible tells us he would not give up his sins for righteousness but spent his days in wild feasts and revelries.

One day Belshazzar made a great feast for his thousand lords and his wives and concubines. They ate and they drank, they danced and they sang a long time and were full of high excitement.

When the gaiety was as its wildest, the king (according to the Bible) cried:

"Arise, go into our temple and bring to me the sacred vessels my father took from the Israelites when he conquered Jerusalem. Bring them to us in our hall so that I and my wives and concubines and princesses may drink from them the wine from our grapes."

The holy vessels were brought, and the servants filled them with red wine, and the king and the princesses and the wives and the concubines drank it. Thus they defiled those vessels, for they were to be used only for the holy Israelite sacraments by the rightfully anointed priests.

"Let the Israelites know," shouted the king, "that we can use their sacred vessels for our feasts as they can use them in their temples. Our gods, made by our workmen of gold and silver and bronze and iron and stone, are stronger than their God." Thus they mocked and shouted and kept on drinking.

While all this noisy clanging and clattering and blasphemous derision was going on, there suddenly came forth from the white wall a hand with fingers!

Silence fell on the great chamber and lo, the great multitude, the king, princes, lords, and ladies turned pale with fear! The oil lamps and candles became dim, and the fingers of that strange hand began writing over against the candlesticks upon the plaster of the wall of the king's palace. The fingers of the hand wrote slowly and clearly.

The king's countenance became ashen in color and his knees knocked one against the other while the hand wrote slowly and clearly the words: *mene, mene, tekel, upharsin.*

Then the hand was gone! But the deadly silence remained.

Slowly the oil lamps grew brighter and the candles shone stronger, and slowly speech came back to the company of frightened revelers. Questions were tossed around and there was much guessing, but no one knew the words or their meaning.

In the end King Belshazzar cried aloud: "Bring the astrologers, the Chaldeans, and the soothsayers. Whosoever shall read this writing and show me the interpretation thereof, he shall be clothed in scarlet and shall have a chain of gold about his neck and shall be the third ruler of the kingdom."

The order went forth and the wise men came, but they could not understand the writing nor could they interpret it.

King Belshazzar was deeply troubled. His face showed fear, and the princes and nobles were disturbed.

When the queen saw this she came to the king and spake: "O King, live forever! Let not thy thoughts trouble thee. There is a man in thy kingdom, an Israelite captured by your father, in whom is the spirit of the holy God. He showed great wisdom and knowledge in the days of thy father, who made him master of the magicians, astrologers, the Chaldeans, and the soothsayers. His name is Daniel. Now let Daniel be called and he will read the writing and make known the interpretation thereof."

Then was Daniel brought before the king, and the

king spake and said unto Daniel: "I have heard that thou art of the children of the captivity of Judah whom my father brought out of Jewry, and I have heard that the spirit of the gods is in thee. There is a handwriting on the wall that my astrologers can neither understand nor interpret. I have heard that thou canst make interpretations and dissolve doubts. And I have heard that the spirit of God is in thee and that thou hast wisdom and understanding. Therefore read me this writing and tell me the interpretation thereof. Then thou shalt be clothed in scarlet and thou shalt have a chain of gold about thy neck and shalt be third ruler in the kingdom."

Then Daniel answered: "O thou King, the most high God gave Nebuchadnezzar, thy father, a kingdom, and majesty, and glory and honor. But when his heart was lifted up, his mind hardened in pride and he worshiped idols. He lost his throne. He was turned into a beast of the field and he lived among the beasts in the field until he knew that the most high God ruled the kingdom of men.

"And thou, O Belshazzar, thou didst know all this. Yet thou hast not humbled thy heart and dost worship false gods of gold and silver, bronze and iron and wood and stone which see not nor hear nor understand.

"Thy servants brought the sacred vessels which thy father, the king, took from the temple of Jerusalem, and thou and thy nobles and thy wives and thy concubines defiled them by drinking from them. So He sent the hand to write the writing and this is what it says: *mene, mene, tekel, upharsin.*

"And this is the interpretation of the words. *Mene:* God has numbered thy kingdom and finished it.

"*Tekel:* Thou art weighed in the balance of heaven and art found wanting.

"*Peres:** Thy kingdom will be divided and will be given to the Medes and the Persians."

In that night was Belshazzar the king of Chaldeans slain, and his kingdom was taken by Darius, king of the Medes. This is the tale as related in the Bible.

Thus, the balance of the zodiac in the heavens was ever used in judgment of the deeds of kings and men upon earth.

* This is the same word as *upharsin* in a different tense.

SCORPIUS
THE SCORPION

It is strange that perhaps the most brilliant stars in all the zodiac—those in the constellation Scorpius—are considered the most evil and the most accursed in the great heavenly belt. For Scorpius—the ancient symbol of gloom and death—ever foretold tragedy and calamity, and plagues of insects and locusts and reptiles.

The appearance of these stars brought with it cold, darkness, and bleak winter, because in those ancient times the sun rose and set with Scorpius during the period from October 24 to November 22, when warm, sunny days were no more. Strong winds, little sun, shivering cold were and still are the order of these days.

Add to this the fact that Scorpius was considered a sign of war, for the birth of Mars, the Roman god of war, fell in this period.

Scorpius is known as one of the very oldest constellations. There are records of it in 5000 B.C. as a sign of horror and evil. It is found in the oldest epic known to us: the epic of Gilgamesh. In it are monsters, half scorpion and half man. They were so terrible and poisonous that even to look at them meant death. It was the very ancient goddess Tiamat who came out of the vast space and created these fierce creatures, whose heads touched heaven and whose poison scorpion tails touched hell.

The most brilliant star in the constellation of Scorpius is named Antares. Great, gleaming, and nearly blood red in color, truly a giant glittering evil eye in heaven, it brings death and destruction to nature and man. The Mayas, the people of Central America, called it the sign of "the Death God." The only people who had a good word for that part of the zodiac were the old alchemists, for, they said, in that period iron can be most easily changed into gold.

In far hidden times, it is said, there were only six zodiacal constellations recognized by the astronomers, and Scorpius was one of them. How could they not see that bright bloody red star in heaven opposite another glorious shining star in Orion, which stood for warmth, growth, and sunshine?

Scorpius is the one zodiacal constellation that really looks like the creature whose name it bears: a scorpion. Antares, the blood-glowing star, is the heart, the center. A long curving arc of stars is behind it, seemingly ending in a group of stars, sharply curving, like the poison stinger of the animal. Above Antares, the heart, there are sweeping, bending stars that make up the upper part of the body and the head and claws of the poisonous creature. These resemble and are commonly designated as the claws. Later on, these claws were designated as the zodiacal sign of Libra.

In Greek mythology it was a scorpion that attacked Orion, the greatest of all hunters. I mentioned the horror of the scorpion men in the days of Gilgamesh in Mesopotamia. Nevertheless, modern star-diviners, astrologers who say that every person's life is shaped by the stars under which he is born, tell a different tale of those born between October and November. These astrologers say those born under the sign of Scorpius have great courage and are often strong, short-necked people. They are believed to have the strength to uphold what is right and to be aggressive.

And they are said to have great self-control and so give strength to those with whom they come in contact.

All in all, Scorpius people are believed to have strong will power and to be full of determination, ready to go into new enterprises and to overcome difficulties.

The topaz is the stone of Scorpius, the red carnation its flower, and vermilion its color.

There are splendid tales told of that poisonous creature, most of them tragic. I have chosen two, one that tells of the sinister meaning of Scorpius and one in which this zodiacal constellation has a happy and bright shining place, even as do the stars themselves.

The Hero
in the Sky

First, the tale of Orion, son of Poseidon, the god of the sea. He was the handsomest and tallest of all the Greeks, and loves came to him like bees to roses.

One day he saw Merope, the daughter of the king of Chios, and fell in love with her. So he came to the king, Merope's father, and said:

"O King, I love your daughter and would take her for my wife."

"Orion, son of Poseidon of the endless sea, men say you are the geratest hunter of Greece. You are worthy of marrying my daughter, but before I give her to you, I would ask you to do a deed for me. My land is cursed with many wild beasts and monsters. Rid me of them and I will give you my daughter for wife."

"That I will do gladly, O King! Your daughter is well worth the labor." And he set himself to the task at once.

At the end of the first day he destroyed many a monster that had brought horror to the land of Chios. When the sun went deep down behind the clouds, he brought the pelts of the beasts to the palace, to the chamber of his beloved Merope.

"Merope, with eyes like the stars in the heaven, here are the pelts of the wild creatures I slew today. Soon your father's land will be clear of them and then there will be the great celebration of our wedding day."

"I knew you would do the task my father gave you, and I await with joy the day when you will be finished."

Each day Orion returned with more pelts, bringing the skins to the palace. When he thought his labor was done, he came before the king. "O King of Chios," he spoke, "your land is free of beasts and monsters. Now I have come for your daughter, whom you promised me."

"There are still lions and wolves and bears in the hills and in the woods. Destroy them and then you may have my daughter."

Orion continued hunting as the king desired, but each time he came for his prize, the king put him off.

One day when Orion felt downhearted because of the king's deceitfulness, he drank too much of the good Chios wine. When his mind was all in a fog, he broke into Merope's chamber and pleaded and told her that she must be his wife.

When the king learned of this, his fury was more

terrible than the monsters of his land. "Orion has committed a woeful crime against me and against my daughter and against my people," cried the king. "It must be avenged, and my father, God Dionysus, must help me." Then he cried unto the high heaven:

"O my father enthroned on lofty Olympus, thou art a god and my father. Come to my aid and help me avenge the outrage Orion committed."

Then the voice of Dionysus was heard from on high: "Son, I hear your plea and I will help you. I will send you my Satyrs. They are half-man and half-beast, and their only pleasure is wild dancing and drinking and singing and playing pranks. Send Orion among them and soon you will be able to avenge the wrong against you."

The wild Satyrs came, and the king said to Orion: "There have come here half-men who are your kind in revelry. They love frolicking as dogs love hunting. You will like them. Go among them and join them in their merrymaking."

Orion joined them, and they danced and drank and sang so they could be heard through hill and dale. The Satyrs made Orion drink more and more, until he was so fast asleep, Zeus's thunder could not wake him.

Then the king of Chios, the father of Merope, did a terrible deed. He blinded the sleeping Orion, the great hunter, and had him taken to the raging sea.

After a time Orion awoke and sat up. Blackness! Emptiness! Emptiness!

"Gods on Olympus!" he cried. "I am blind! I cannot see! I cannot see the blue sky! I cannot see the green

woods! No more will I see the lovely face of Merope! No more can I hunt!

"O ye gods! Why was I so cursed? No more will I see man or beast! Who did this horrible crime to me?"

He kept on crying and weeping and lamenting until he was heard by the gods. And those who favored him sent him the voice of the oracle who sees into the future and foretells events. And these were the soothing words of the oracle:

"Go traveling to the east and turn your empty eyes in the direction of the sun god when he rises from the sea. Then you will be able to see once again as you did."

Orion, the beautiful, the giant, fearless and full of hopeful courage, set out on the sea. Of a sudden he heard in the distance the sounds of a smith's hammering.

"Follow that sound," he said to the sailors. "It is a friendly sound and I know it will bring me help."

The sailors did as they were ordered, and thus Orion came to the island of Lemnos, where there was the smithy of the one-eyed Cyclopses.

The smithy was busy with hammering and clanging. One Cyclops standing in the center, arms raised high, was ordering his apprentices to work. Orion saw none of it, but the sounds were music to his ears.

"Master Smith," Orion said, "you see the beautiful world with your one eye, but I am cursed. I have no eyes and to me there is only darkness. Can you spare one of your apprentices to go with me and help me in my misfortune?"

"How can one of my apprentices help you?"

"He can be my eyes. I must travel to the east with my eyes turned to where the sun god rises from the ocean. Then will I have my sight again."

The Cyclops was sorry for the sightless giant, so he ordered one of his young apprentices, Cedalion by name, to walk with Orion.

"No, he need not walk, for my strides are long and fast," said Orion. "I still have all my strength and I will carry him on my back while he guides me on the way."

So he took the apprentice on his shoulders and began walking to the east where the sun god rises every day.

Orion walked with big strides over hills and through dales, through streams and vales. The apprentice smith sat on his shoulders, his dark eyes wide and searching. So they kept on for days, until one day, when the heat was gone and cool winds were coming up, the boy suddenly shouted:

"Orion, I see the edge of the ocean! We are at the end of our journey!"

"I smell the great water, boy, if only . . ." Orion stopped, for he heard a voice speaking: "Young giant, with a face blessed by the gods, I heard the boy on your shoulders call you Orion. From your face and your stature I take you to be Orion, the great hunter and the comeliest man in Greece. I am Eos, the sister of the sun god."

"Thanks unto the gods," cried Orion, "for I have reached the end of my journey. I am Orion the hunter and I was treacherously blinded by the king of Chios. But the oracle told me I will regain my sight when I turn my eyes to the face of the sun god, your brother, when he comes out to greet the ocean. That is why I came here."

"I am saddened at your misfortune, O Orion! And I will plead with my brother to give you back your eyes so that you can see the green water and the great world once again. Wait here for him when he comes up to greet the day."

She returned into the sea, where she spoke to her brother, pleading for the blinded giant.

Orion remained with the boy on his shoulders. "Boy," said he, "don't close your eyes, but keep a close watch to see when the sun god comes from the ocean. Tell me quickly when you see him."

So they waited watchfully and eagerly. Many hours passed; then they suddenly felt a cool breeze streaming from the sea, and that was followed by a streaming, warm, golden light.

"I think the sun god is coming, boy!" shouted Orion. "Look hard and tell me what you see."

Orion strained every muscle in his body and his head and his sightless eyes in the direction from which the warmth came.

The sun god, great, glorious, and shining, came out of the billowing water and Orion knew it.

"Help me, divine Sun God! Help me so I can see the world again!"

"Your wish is granted," spoke the sun god. "You will have your sight again."

And of a sudden Orion could see!

He saw the great, dark-green water before him. He

saw the sky. He saw the golden shining light of the sun god! He was so happy he could hardly speak.

"Thanks! Thanks, O Sun God!" he mumbled.

The sun god went on up to the sky.

"Come, boy," Orion shouted happily, "come, I will carry you back to your smithy." He turned back with giant, strong strides, the boy still on his shoulders. He was thinking hard and clearly: I swear I will have my revenge on him who blinded me! Then, aloud: "I vow when I return you, boy, I will not rest until I have taken revenge on the king of Chios. I will seek him after I bring you back to the smithy."

He came to the smithy and thanked the Cyclopses and thanked the boy. Then he went off to seek the king of Chios.

But the king had heard of Orion's vow and had fled and hidden. Orion could not find him, but he kept on looking.

So, wandering about, he met Artemis, the goddess, who was also a famous huntress. The two became fast friends and hunted together. Great were their deeds in the land, and one day Orion made a big, bragging boast to Artemis.

"I am strong and all men say I am the greatest hunter on earth. I could destroy all the animals on earth if I willed it."

Now, Apollo, brother of Artemis, who was jealous of Orion's strength, heard this and muttered, "So Orion thinks he is more powerful than the gods. Such boasting is unbecoming to mortal creatures. I must destroy that braggart, but I cannot do it alone, so I will ask Mother Earth, who is a friend of the animals that roam in her realm, to help me. Surely she does not want to see all of them destroyed.

"Mother Earth," he cried, "Orion is bragging he will destroy all the animals that roam the fields, now that he has his sight once again. He holds himself greater than we, the gods, who created the animals."

"Such boasting cannot be allowed," said Mother Earth. "I will send one of those he boasts he will destroy to poison him and put an end to him."

She called forth a monster scorpion that had an armor of shell no weapon could penetrate. It had giant pincer claws and a curving body that could turn and twist swift as an arrow. At the end of its body was a poison dart, a stinger that would destroy anything it hit.

"Go forth," Mother Earth said to the scorpion, "go and attack that braggart who said he could annihilate all the animals in the world. Attack him and destroy him."

The scorpion slithered toward Orion.

The giant hero was not scared; he attacked the beast with his sharp arrows. But the arrows did not pierce the monster. Then Orion leaped at the beast, sword in hand, and began hacking at its body and poison tail, but it did the beast no harm. Orion saw he was dealing with a monster that could not be destroyed. So he leaped into the sea to escape. The giant creature followed him, caught up with him, and bit him and stung him in the foot. And so Orion died.

Others tell that Orion died in a different way, but,

whichever was the way, his death brought great sadness among many of the gods and most of all to Artemis, the great huntress who had been with Orion many a moon. She mourned for him without end and then took him with her up into the heaven where she could look at him eternally, and there he has been ever since.

When the monster scorpion saw his victim high up in heaven, he rushed up to pursue him there.

So when you look up into the sky, you will see Orion, the great hero giant, a lionskin over his left arm and his giant club in his right hand, with his two hunting dogs by his side. And there is also the Scorpion, in the zodiacal constellation following, ready to attack him, but never reaching him. . . .

The Great Magic
Fish of Maui

And now I will tell you a tale of Scorpius that pierces through the darkness of misfortune usually associated with that constellation. This is a tale of the far, far-away time when the world had just begun for the people of distant Polynesia.

There was only vast space: Ranga, heaven, was the upper part, and Papa, earth, was the lower. They were one, together. All was deep gray-blue shadows. Sometimes there was a rolling and surging in the silent world.

Father Heaven, Ranga, and Mother Earth, Papa, had children who lived in that whispering twilight of darkness, and they did not like it.

"Our parents must be separated; they must be separated."

"We must have free space. Father Ranga must be high up, far above, and Mother Earth must be here below, touching our bodies as a mother should."

First one son tried. He forced his way in between them and pushed and pressed with shoulders and arms, but he made no progress. They were still one, together.

The next son tried; he forced and heaved with shoulders and arms and back, but he could do no more than the one before.

Then the third tried, Tane-Mahuta, father and god of the forests, birds, and insects, and with his great strength he slowly, slowly separated them.

At that, all the children who had lived in the dark roamed freely wherever they wanted. A few of those children had human shapes and from them descended Maui of the many names, who was destined to be a great hero.

Maui had four brothers. He was the smallest of the five and they never saw him. Even his own mother did not remember him.

One night when his mother and brothers were together to dance in the great meetinghouse, the mother called only each of her four sons. Then little Maui came forth.

"Mother, why didn't you call me, your fifth son?" he said.

"I do not know you."

"Even if you don't, I am still your son, even though you have forgotten me. When I was born, you wrapped me in the black hair taken from the top of your head and threw me into the white waves. Seaweeds covered me and there I lived until the wind brought me onto the sand of the beach.

"Soft jellyfish covered me to protect me, but the flies laid their eggs in me and the birds pecked at me and I was only saved by my great ancestor Tama-nui-ki-te-Rangi. I lived with him until I felt a great call to see you and my father and brothers, and here I am."

The mother and the brothers looked at him and they knew he told the truth.

"Now I remember you," said his mother, "and I will call you Maui-tiki-tiki-O-Taranga, Maui raised in the topknot hair of Taranga, your mother."

From then on they lived together, Maui performing all kinds of deeds and playing all kinds of tricks. He also could perform all sorts of magic, especially after he got the marvelous magic jawbone from his ancestress Muri-ranga-whenua.

His brothers were a little afraid of his trickiness, and when they went on long fishing trips, they would not take him along. One day they planned such a trip and did not say a word to him. But Maui, because of his magic power, knew of their plans and decided he would go along just the same. He made himself a fishhook from a piece of the magic jawbone of his ancestress, and he chanted the proper prayers over it, to give it great magic power. Then he hid under the slats of the floor of the canoe.

The brothers set out, and when they were far away from the land, Maui crept out from under the floor.

When his brothers saw him, they wanted to return

at once, but Maui, with his magic spells, widened the sea so that the land was too far away for them to return.

The brothers fished, and soon they had a boatful and wanted to return.

"Now I will fish," said Maui, "and I will bring up the biggest fish man ever brought from these waters!"

He brought out his magic fishhook from under his *maro*, the cloth he wore around his body. It was the most beautiful fishhook ever seen.

"Brothers, look at this fishhook; there is in it a piece of the magic jawbone and it is decorated with the hair of a dog's tail. Give me some bait and I will bring up a fish the like of which has never been seen in our islands."

"If you have a magic fishhook, you can get bait in a magic way," they answered.

Maui laughed and shouted, "If that is the way you feel, I will be the bait for that wonderfish!" He began pummeling his nose until the red blood ran from it. Then he smeared the magic fishhook with it, let it dry, and with a wide motion of his arm and magic songs from his throat, tossed it into the sea. His arm moved back and forth, and the spell of his magic song cut through the sunny green waves.

Down, down, down went that charmed fishhook through the green water until it caught something soft and wound its way around it.

Maui began drawing up the line, pulling hard and heavy.

"It must be my giant fish," Maui shouted.

He pulled harder and harder. The canoe tilted to one side and the water poured into it.

The brothers shouted: "Drop the line or we'll all drown."

"Bail harder," Maui shouted back, and braced his feet against the canoe. "Bail harder; I won't let go what my magic hook has caught."

He kept on pulling and chanting charm songs. He knew his hook had caught the roof of a house deep in the sea.

Slowly it came up in the swaying water.

Maui eased his line and down went all into the sea! But he began pulling faster, shouting his spell and song words. And so strong was the magic of his song that the giant catch came up again, and with it the houses and the land all around. Fires were burning, birds flew in the air, dogs ran along the grass and trees, and people were at work at their daily tasks.

"Here is a great fish I brought from the sea with my magic fishhook," cried Maui to his brothers. "Now I will go to the village and give thanks to the gods and give to them what belongs to them. Don't eat any of the fish until that is done and I return." And he went off.

No sooner was he gone than his brothers did what he told them *not* to do. This made the gods angry, and Maui's giant fish tossed wildly around, and it made the land jagged and mountainous. Today people call that land New Zealand.

When the great father sun looked at the big new land, the fish of Maui became hard and solid as it is today.

The Maoris, who live there today, say the northern part of the island is shaped like and is the fish of Maui, and the southern part is the canoe in which Maui and his brothers rode.

And the wise men say Maui was so happy and proud of the "fish" he had brought up from the sea that he threw the magic fishhook high up into the sky and the stars gathered around it and have stayed there ever since, and the people on the earth called those stars Scorpius.

SAGITTARIUS
THE ARCHER

The ninth in the stardom of the zodiac is Sagittarius, the great Archer in history, legend, and astronomy. The history of this constellation is somewhat different from any of the others, for there are two Archers, as you will learn later. But first I want to tell you a little about the history and position of Sagittarius, which also relates to its folklore.

Now, Sagittarius the Archer is really the figure of a centaur, that mythical creature half-horse and half-man.

This constellation lies west of Capricornus, with its arrow ever aiming straight at Scorpius, which lies to the west of the Archer. The horse's part, the hoofs, rest in the richest part of the Milky Way.

These stars were already known in very ancient times. The Chinese worshiped them three thousand years before the Christian era, and in India there are records, also going back over three thousand years before Christ, likening these stars to a horse's head.

Often Sagittarius is also called the Bull Killer, for when he rises, Taurus sets.

Here are a few words about the centaurs. They came to Greece from the far cold north where there were the great cloud-horses of the sun. Those who tamed them loved them and desired the strength of these heavenly horses so much that they became part of them. Thus the centaurs came to be half-horse and half-human. That is what the old tales tell us.

The greatest and best-known of these centaurs was Chiron. He was perfect in the arts taught to him by two gods, Apollo and Artemis. He was a fine musician, a great healer, and an excellent huntsman. And he was also blessed with the gift of prophecy. Many a famous man and great hero owed his knowledge to Chiron. Among them were Aesculapius, the father of ancient medicine; Heracles, the most famous of heroes, and many others.

The ancients also tell that Chiron arranged the stars in heaven in their proper places so that people would be guided by them in their voyages and the seasons would come in the right time and order.

I said before that there is a difference between the ninth and the other zodiacal constellations, and this is the difference. There are two Archers in the sky; the other is called Centaurus and is in the southern part of the heavens. The tale that follows will tell you how it came to be there.

Astrology has many good words about those born under the sign of the Archer, that is, between November 23 and December 22.

First, there is a religious Christian meaning in Sagittarius ever aiming his arrow at Scorpius. It is a symbolic meaning of the good angel slaying Satan, who is forever tempting mankind.

As for those born under this famous constellation, they are said to be under the protection of heaven and to follow the spirit of truth and righteousness.

The men are believed to be full of courage and good judges of character, with gifts of the highest qualities: wisdom and foresight.

Astrology also describes them as happy, jovial, frank, and of a positive nature. Since they are said to have intense, active minds, they look to their own affairs without outside help.

The women are said to be fine home-bodies, to keep to their own affairs, to be bright in conversation, and very reliable.

The carbuncle is the gem of the sign, though some say it is the amethyst. The color is yellow, and the flower is the goldenrod.

Why There Are Two Centaurs in the Sky

The great tale of Sagittarius the Archer is the one about his deeds in heaven and how he got there to stay forever.

Chiron was a centaur different from all the other centaurs. Instead of being wild and boisterous, he was gentle and wise.

The grandchild of Ixion and a cloud, which Zeus had turned into a woman, he proved different from his very birth, showing a great interest in knowledge and in helping others. He became known far and wide for his wisdom and as a teacher. Soon famous heroes of those days sent their children to be taught by him, and some of the greatest men of antiquity learned what they knew from Chiron.

He also showed a keen understanding of the art of war. Achilles and even Heracles, he who performed the twelve most daring deeds of ancient times, they and many others were said to have studied with him.

One day Heracles came to visit Pholus the centaur, who was his friend. They spoke of this and that, as friends do when they meet. Then Heracles said: "Friend Pholus, I traveled a long and dusty way and I would welcome a drink of cool wine."

"Friend Heracles," Pholus replied, "I have no wine of my own save what we centaurs all own and drink together."

"Pholus, we have been friends for a long time and we have hunted and feasted together often. Your brother centaurs know that and surely won't object if you give me some wine."

Pholus liked Heracles, and so he went into the cave where the wine of the centaurs was stored in clay jars standing on tripods and chose the oldest, the one he thought the best wine, and brought it out.

He broke the seal and opened the top of the jar. The wine had been there a long time and was rich and strong, and the aroma of it spread quickly in all directions.

Pholus poured two large cups, one for himself and one for his friend, and the perfume of the good wine spread like an early spring breeze floating far and wide and reaching into the woods where the centaurs were disporting themselves. They smelled the wine perfume.

"Who has opened our wine jars, which can only be done when we are all together?" they shouted. "It must be a thief or robber. We'll make him pay for this."

With their heavy hoofs pounding the ground, they rushed to where the two friends were drinking peacefully.

When Heracles saw them racing wildly toward him, with a roar that could be heard as far as the sea, he thought they were coming to attack him. He leaped up and let loose his arrows poisoned with the monster Hydra's gall. Then he began laying about him with his club.

"Stop battling! Cease shooting arrows!" Pholus roared. "Heracles is my friend and I gave him a welcome cup of our wine when he came to visit me!"

Good Chiron, who came with the roaring centaurs, stood a way off with sorrow on his face.

"Why must there always be war and slaughter when there could be peace and good will? Here they are battling without any cause at all, only a misunderstanding."

Heracles and the centaurs hardly heard Chiron's pleading because of the shouting and shooting and spear-throwing and club-swinging. Then, little by little, the turmoil ceased and the centaurs understood that Pholus and Heracles had been sitting together as friends. But horror! When they became quiet they found that one of Heracles's poisoned arrows had accidentally struck Chiron, who had been sorrowing over the battle.

Great was the grief of all the centaurs and of Heracles at the terrible news. For to be struck by an arrow that had on it the dried poisoned gall of the monster Hydra meant death. But Chiron was immortal. The poison could not kill him, yet it caused him terrible pain.

CAPRICORNUS
THE GOAT-FISH

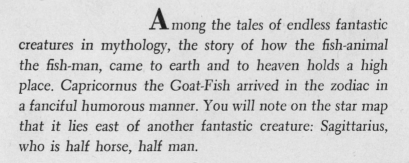

Among the tales of endless fantastic creatures in mythology, the story of how the fish-animal the fish-man, came to earth and to heaven holds a high place. Capricornus the Goat-Fish arrived in the zodiac in a fanciful humorous manner. You will note on the star map that it lies east of another fantastic creature: Sagittarius, who is half horse, half man.

The pain was so fierce and piercing that Chiron wished he were dead. But die he could not. He tried on himself all the arts of medicine he knew, but it was of no use. Every minute the pain grew worse. Chiron could not stand it.

"O Zeus!" he cried in agony. "I do not want to be immortal. I want to die rather than suffer this awful agony for which there is no cure! I want to die! Take my immortality from me and save me from this cruel suffering!"

Zeus heard the cries of distress. "I will grant you your desire, Chiron!" he said, and with that Chiron became mortal and died!

The centaurs were deeply saddened and so were the gods, Zeus most of all.

"You brought wisdom and peace to the world," he lamented, "and now I will set you in the heaven so that all the world can look at you forever and remember your wisdom and goodness."

But when Zeus looked at the sky where Chiron had already arranged the stars in fine and proper order in the northern sphere, he saw there was no place for Chiron himself in that sphere. So he set him instead in the southern part, where great Chiron, known as Centaurus, is there for all the world to see and remember for his fine virtues.

Thus there are two centaurs in the sky; one of them is Sagittarius, arranged by Chiron, and the other is Centaurus, set there by Zeus.

Although not so bright as its neighbor, nor as noticeable, the Goat was important in the zodiac millenniums ago, way back in prehistoric times. In Oriental legends Capricornus was nurse to the young sun god, one of the oldest gods in the world.

In studying the prehistoric records in stone and metal, we meet again and again half-of-one-kind, half-of-another-kind creatures. There is the sphinx, half woman, half lion, with a serpent's or lion's tail; there are the centaurs, half man, half horse; there are the mermaids and the mermen, half human, half fish; there are also the Egyptian gods: animal heads and human bodies, and many others. Capricornus is often mentioned in ancient records because it was held that when the souls left human bodies, they went up to heaven through the stars of Capricornus, and so this constellation was often called "the Gate of the Gods." (When souls came from heaven into human bodies, they went through the stars of Cancer.)

The name Capricornus probably originated with the Babylonians, as did the names of most of the constellations. Some claim it originated with the Sumerians, the nation that existed before the Babylonian and that had an important place in ancient religion.

The idea of two creatures in one perhaps began with the great belief in the "two-ness" of the very ancient god Ea of Mesopotamia. Ea was a most important deity who had two distinct ways of existence. He was the god of the underground fresh water and springs, and fresh water was even more important in ancient times than it is today. At night Ea descended to his underground sweet waters, and in the day he was among men and gods, always doing good for both. For he was a kindly god, never angry, never battling, always helping those in need of help.

Ea was called the antelope of the waters, and he was usually represented as part antelope and part fish.

Capricornus was favored by Ea; perhaps Capricornus was an outgrowth of Ea, becoming a horned goat with a fish's tail. Sometimes he was called the fish-ram, and there are representations of Ea as a ram.

The Capricornus constellation is made up of two pairs of stars and a series of stars in a curve that, with a stretch of imagination, can be considered the body of a goat ending in the fish tail.

Astrologers say those born under the sign of Capricornus, from December 23 to January 20, are in the kingdom of universal order and perfection.

Those born then are said to have a fine moral character, to undertake serious responsibilities, and have great respect for what people think of them.

Astrologers also say they are steadfast and reliable, natural leaders, and good organizers in whatsoever they undertake.

With all these qualities Capricorns are full of ambition for power and wealth. Unfortunately they are very sensitive, and this leads them to worry about the actions and attitudes of their friends.

Those born under the Goat-Fish, it is said, are subject to many illnesses.

Women born at that time are very sensible, and often they are better managers than men, planning carefully and arranging their work systematically. They are not very talkative, and order all they do with few words. Astrologers call Capricornus a feminine sign.

The stone for these days is the chalcedony, and the flower is the snowdrop. The color is vermilion or russet.

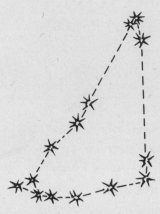

The Laughing
Zodiac
in the Sky

The ancient Greek gods were often battling gigantic half gods or other gods to gain power and rule lands and people.

Zeus, the chief god of the Greeks, had been in many such wars. He had destroyed numbers of the giant demigods and often imprisoned others who opposed him. This angered Mother Earth, who was also the mother of the half-divine Titans. To avenge herself she wedded one of these Titans, Tartarus by name, and with him she had a son who was the most frightful giant that ever existed. They called him Typhon.

From his thighs down Typhon's body was poisonous

snakes. His arms were the longest in the world, reaching a hundred leagues in all directions. His hands were poison serpents like his body below his thighs. He had the head of a wild ass that reached as far as the stars, and there were wings on his shoulders large enough to shut off the light of the sun from the earth. Fire came from his eyes, and when he roared, flaming rocks came from his mouth.

This monster was as terrible in thoughts and deeds as he was in body. He destroyed everything he touched.

On a day when his thoughts were more black than the blackest night, he roared to Mother Earth: "I will avenge the death of my brother Titans. They were destroyed by Zeus and those who are with him on Mount Olympus. Now I will destroy them. I will make dust and rubble out of them!"

Madly, Typhon the monster rushed through the world to Mount Olympus where the gods lived.

The gods on Mount Olympus heard the roaring of the monster from afar and saw the frightening destruction as he flew along.

"Fly! Save yourself," Zeus shouted. "That monster is stronger than we are. Fly! Hide wherever you can!"

The gods fled wildly through the air, over mountains and waters, with Typhon after them, spitting flaming rocks from his mouth in all directions. The sun was hidden by the giant's wings, and everything far and near was scorched.

The Greek gods flew on helter-skelter until they reached the land of Egypt, but the monster was not far away.

"We must hide ourselves in the disguise of animals so that Typhon does not find us," thundered Zeus.

No sooner were the words out of his godly mouth than he changed himself into a ram. Hera, the wife of

Zeus, turned into a white cow; Ares, the son of Zeus, into a boar; Apollo, the god of music and dance, turned into a crow. All the gods turned into animals and fled in all directions around the Nile River.

Among the deities was one, Pan, a merry god of woods and fields who became bewildered in the rush and excitement and noise. He had horns on his head like a goat and goat's hoofs for feet.

He couldn't make up his mind how to change. So, since he had goat horns on his head, he changed the upper part of his body into a goat, and since his hoof-feet were in the waters of the Nile, he changed his lower body into a fish tail. Then he hid as the other gods had.

Typhon did not find Zeus. But the battle between him and the other gods continued, and in the end Zeus, having lost his fear, changed back into his former shape, battled the monster, and defeated him. He hurled Mount Aetna at him, burying him under it. That is why fire has been coming out of Mount Aetna ever since. It is the fiery breath of Typhon.

The gods all returned to Mount Olympus in their former shapes, and there was much talk about how Pan became bewildered standing in the Nile River and how comical he looked in his disguise of half goat and half fish tail.

Zeus and all the gods thought Pan's disguise was very funny.

Said Zeus: "I'll put Pan's funny disguise into the sky for all the world to see and for all the world to enjoy as a merry sight.

"We and all the world can laugh at it to the end of time."

So Zeus took stars and formed Capricornus the Goat-Fish in the heavens, and it has been there ever since.

AQUARIUS
THE WATER CARRIER

The zodiacal constellation Aquarius is definitely connected with water, the sea. There are also other zodiacal constellations that are related to that element. Water is one of the very important and rich gifts in the world, and so there are endless tales about water in mythology and life.

The season of rains comes during the days when Aquarius rules in the sky, and so that part of the zodiac is said to be responsible for it.

The ancient Chaldeans believed the portion of the sky that is ruled by Aquarius the Water-Carrier was a great heavenly sea, and so they called that area "the Sea." In it were two more constellations: Capricornus and Pisces.

Two of them, Aquarius and Capricornus, were linked with the good god Ea, of whom I told you in a previous chapter.

Aquarius the Water-Carrier lies between the Goat-Fish and Pisces the Fishes. He, it was said, had most control of this particular region. He was always represented as a boy or as a mature man holding an urn from which came a never-ending flow of water for the welfare of mankind—or sometimes for its destruction. In some of the images found of him the water flowed from a large bucket or from his body, and he was also known as the Water-Pourer. Such figures of him have been found dating back fifteen hundred years before the Christian era.

In Egypt it was believed that the setting of Aquarius, which coincides with the rising of Sirius, the Dog Star, which is the brightest star in the sky, caused the rising of the river Nile. It was Aquarius sinking into the shallow Nile with his giant water urn that added the water that caused the river to rise.

Some peoples considered Aquarius a heavenly benefactor who brought water for the growth of food. But others, where Aquarius brought floods and destruction and cold, feared his coming. Some three thousand years ago the sun was at its lowest and weakest point when it was in Aquarius. It was the time of the winter solstice, and the days were dark and cold.

Astrology has many good things to say for those born under Aquarius, January 21 to February 19.

They are said to have keen minds, to be accurate in their judgment, quick in discussion, and to have progressive, agreeable, and courteous manners. Astrologers also say Aquarians are calm and peaceful, their reasoning clear, and they are good judges of character.

Although most of the time they are calm and patient, Aquarians have some faults, but these can easily be corrected. Often they do not keep their promises and are apt to be headstrong and capricious.

Women born under Aquarius are said to have high social ambitions and to be witty, bright, and lively. They have good common sense and are attached to home and their families.

But Aquarius is thought to be mostly a masculine sign that brings good fortune.

Its precious stone is the amethyst, its flower is the primrose, and its color sea blue.

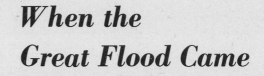

When the
Great Flood Came

There is no end to the ways of telling a great, world-wide tale, and now I will tell you one that has been told in hundreds of ways for many, many thousands of years.

Of the four elements in the world that give life to mankind, water has perhaps been the most important. It is therefore natural that Aquarius the Water Carrier and his giant urn come up in one form or another in all the lands of the world.

In Greece, Aquarius was sometimes known as, or identified with, Deucalion, son of Prometheus the Titan. In his time the never-ending water coming from the heavenly urn drowned the whole world.

The tale goes thus:

Zeus, the chief god of the Greeks, saw men in the world growing more and more wicked. He saw them committing crimes against one another and waging bloody wars. He saw them living in dishonesty and robbing one another, and it filled him with sadness and anger.

"Why can't they be good and generous and kind?" he thundered. But they were not; they became worse as time went on. In the end Zeus thundered forth:

"I will destroy the sinful men of this terrible world. I will cleanse the valleys and mountains of them, I will cleanse the fields and woods of them, for, wherever they come, they bring destruction and ruin."

He decided to destroy mankind with the very element that brought them food: water!

"I will let loose upon them such floods of water that no creature will be left living."

The gods heard the terrible decree and felt as Zeus did.

At that time Deucalion, king of Phthia, was visiting his father Prometheus the Titan in the Caucasus, who also heard of the coming great flood.

"Son," said he, "Zeus in righteous anger has decided to destroy sinful man on this earth. If you want to be saved, you must build an ark of strong wood for yourself in which you can live. But you must take a few animals and food for many days. Only in that way will you escape the terrible flood that is coming."

"I thank you, my father, for your wise warning and will do what you told me to do. I and my wife, Queen Pyrrha, will live in the ark when the flood comes."

"Start at once," Prometheus said. Deucalion set to work and built an ark of stout wood. He took food for a long journey, and he took some animals. They all went at once into the ark, for the rain had begun.

Water had begun pouring from the sky in fierce torrents, as if from giant buckets. There was endless thunder and lightning, and the noise of the falling water was like the hissing of hordes of snakes and the roaring of thousands of bulls.

The water came down as if the world-wide bucket of Aquarius raced everywhere upside down, letting out all the water of the world on all mankind on the earth.

Waters ran wildly from rivers and waterways, and storm and tempest kept on raging like the sounds of millions of frenzied bees.

The roaring rain kept on for days and days until all mortals had drowned and all the mountains and forests and valleys and cities and plains were flooded with water. The only things seen were the highest peaks of the highest mountains and the wooden ark of Deucalion.

When it seemed that no man was left, the wild rain and storm quieted down. Then the king sent out a dove he had in the ark to see if the storm had ended.

The dove returned with the news that the rains had stopped everywhere and that some trees could be seen.

For nine more days the ark floated around while the waters fell lower. Then it came to rest on Mount Aetna. (Some say it was Mount Athos.) Then King Deucalion and his wife left the ark and came to a temple covered with green seaweed. The stone altar was nearly down.

There the two kneeled down and prayed humbly to Zeus.

"O almighty God," they cried, "you who in your just anger punished mankind for their sins, be forgiving and let them return to earth to live good lives and worship you."

Zeus heard their pleading prayer. Then the greatest of the gods spoke to Hermes, who was the messenger to the gods: "Go to Deucalion and Pyrrha, his wife, and tell them I have heard their prayer and I will grant them their request. A new people will be born to bring life to the land."

Hermes flew to the temple where the two were still kneeling.

"Arise," Hermes said to them. "Arise! Zeus has heard your prayers, which came from your hearts, and will grant your request."

Deucalion and Pyrrha were overjoyed at the news, and they thanked Hermes over and over again. And Hermes returned to Olympus.

No sooner was he gone than there appeared before Deucalion and Pyrrha Themis, one of the Titans and a half goddess who sat next to Zeus on Olympus.

Said she: "Deucalion and Pyrrha, Zeus sent me to instruct you and tell you what to do to bring mankind back to earth. Walk through the land with shrouded heads. Then pick up the bones of your mother and throw them behind you." With these words she was gone.

"Husband," said Pyrrha to Deucalion, "I do not understand the words Themis spoke. My mother is dead long ago and I do not know where her bones are."

"Wife," replied Deucalion, "Themis's words were strange, but I think I know the meaning of what she said. Isn't the earth the mother of all of us, and aren't stones her bones? I believe Themis means for us to throw the stones of Mother Earth lying along the river banks behind us."

"Maybe you are right, husband," the queen said. "Let us do this."

They shrouded their heads as Themis had ordered them, and then, as they walked along, they picked up the stones lying along the river banks and threw them over their shoulders.

Then a wonderful thing happened! The rocks that Deucalion threw over his shoulders took on the forms of men, while the stones Pyrrha threw over her shoulders turned into women.

And so people once again came into the world that had been destroyed by great floods of water.

The ancient Greeks believe that Deucalion was really Aquarius the Water-Carrier in the zodiacal belt, for only he could pour out enough water from his giant, never-drying urn to destroy all the world.

PISCES
THE FISHES

When we come to the last zodiacal constellation, Pisces the Fishes, we find that it is still in the area the ancients called "the Sea." It has an unusual shape and is truly a water and rain sign. Two fairly bright stars, widely separated in the sky, are its distinctive features. Its northeastern star lies quite near the constellation called Andromeda, which is north of the zodiac.

Some of the ancients called this northeastern star a monster sent to devour Andromeda. The southwestern star lies somewhat in the direction of Aquarius.

Later, when the first day of spring occurred while the sun was in Pisces the Fishes, those stars were called "the leaders of the Celestial Host."

Between the two main stars there are groups of faint stars in the shape of a V with long ribbony groups of dim stars connected with the main ones.

Pisces brings with it storms, rains, and shipwrecks at sea. It is the zodiacal constellation that is said to have control of the men who sail the seas.

The ancient Israelites assigned the stars of Pisces to Simon and Levi, whose reputation was for fighting and strife. At the same time they were also the national emblem of the Jews.

Pisces the Fishes also had an important place in the lore of Christianity. The fish has always been a symbol of the Christian faith and the sign of the apostle Saint Matthias. And of course the miracle of the fishes, with which Jesus fed the multitude, has an important place in the Christian religion.

Astrologers claim that Pisces the Fishes is a feminine constellation and that it points to strength and endurance.

Those born under that sign (February 20 to March 21) are said to have a fine perception of color and are often skillful artists, disliking vulgarity and coarseness. And, generally, they are believed to be quiet and patient and peaceful.

Astrologers also believe Pisces people are lofty-minded, are clear-thinking and clear-minded, with fine ideals, and are keen observers and admire intellect. They are said to have a boundless possibility for doing good deeds in the world. Always seeking knowledge, trustworthy and reliable, they forge ahead in life.

But, like all human beings, they have some faults. At times they are boastful, fretful, and impatient. Often wavering and overanxious, they suffer in mind and body. Nevertheless, they have the ability to overcome these faults and make fine progress.

Women born under Pisces are considered very capable and able to assume serious responsibilities. They love their homes and family life.

Pisces influences the health of the feet and ankles. Its gem is the white chrysolite, its flower the daffodil, and its color glistening white. Others say its color is sea blue.

✳

How the Fishes Came to Heaven

I have told you in the tale under the zodiacal constellation Capricornus that the great Greek god Zeus and all the other gods of Mount Olympus fled when Typhon, the most terrible monster that was ever in the world, tried to destroy them. I told you that they were frightened and fled wildly until they came to Egypt and its great Nile River. There they became too tired to go on, afraid that Typhon would soon reach them.

"Change swiftly into animals so that no one will recognize you and hide quickly so that Typhon the monster cannot see you," Zeus commanded. Each god and goddess hastened to follow Zeus's order.

Now, among the host of Greek gods there was Aphrodite (Venus), the goddess of love and beauty, and

Eros (Cupid), her son, the boy god of love who was ever by his mother's side. The mother said to her son:

"Come, Son," she cried, "we must change quickly so the terrible monster does not recognize us and cannot find us."

"Into what kind of animals shall we change, Mother?" said the boy.

"O Son," spoke the goddess, "we are by the great river Nile. Why not change into fishes swimming in the life-giving water? The monster will never know who we are and we can easily hide besides."

At once the goddess of beauty and her lovely son with his bow and arrow changed into two glowing, scaled fishes, both gliding through the green water.

They swam swiftly away while Typhon, the ugliest monster ever known, flew around in wildly raging fury in search of his victims.

The two god-fishes, Aphrodite and Eros, left the water and returned to Mount Olympus. And the two gleaming fishes who helped hide the gods were also taken up into the sky as a reward and placed there to shine forever as the constellation Pisces.*

---

* The Greeks, on the other hand, said that the two Gods Aphrodite and Eros became fishes who "were placed in the zodiac."

BIBLIOGRAPHY

ALLEN, RICHARD H. *Star Names: Their Lore and Meaning*. Rev. ed. New York: Dover, 1963.

ALTER, DINSMORE; CLEMINSHAW, CLARENCE H.; and PHILLIPS, JOHN G. *Pictorial Astronomy*. 3rd rev. ed. New York: Crowell, 1969.

Astrological Magazine, The. Published monthly, 1907–09. Edited by B. Suryanarain Row, Madras.

BAKER, ROBERT H. *An Introduction to Astronomy*. 4th ed. New York: Van Nostrand, 1952.

BEALS, CARLYLE S. *The Uneasy Equilibrium of Our Physical Universe*. University lectures, No. 20. Saskatoon: University of Saskatchewan, 1969.

BEET, ERNEST A. *The Sky and Its Mysteries*. London: Bell, 1952.

BRYAN, CARL R. *The Zodiacal Bible*. Los Angeles: DeVorss, 1935.

BULFINCH, THOMAS. *Mythology*. Rev. and enl. ed. New York: Crowell, 1913.

Chinese Astrology.

DHORME, ÉDOUARD P. *Les Religions de Babylonie et d'Assyrie*. Paris: Presses Universitaires de France, 1945.

Earth and Space. Maplewood, N.J.: Hammond, 1970.

ELGIE, JOSEPH H. *Star and Weather Gossip Concerning the Heavens, the Atmosphere, the Sea*. London: The Author, 1915.

FAGAN, CYRIL. *Zodiacs Old and New*. London: Anscombe, 1951.

FRAZER, JAMES G. *The Golden Bough: A Study in Magic and Religion*. 2 vols. London: Macmillan, 1890.

GASTER, THEODOR H. *Thespis: Ritual, Myth and Drama in the Ancient Near East*. New York: Schuman, 1950.

GLEADOW, RUPERT. *The Origin of the Zodiac*. New York: Atheneum, 1969.

GRAVES, ROBERT. *The Greek Myths*. London: Penguin, 1969.

GRAY, LOUIS H., ed. *The Mythology of All Races*. 13 vols. New York: Cooper, 1964. Vol. 1: *Greek and Roman*, by William S. Fox. Vol. 3: *Celtic*, by John A. MacCulloch; *Slavic*, by Jan Máchal. Vol. 5: *Semitic*, by Stephen H. Langdon. Vol. 6:

Indian, by A. Berriedale Keith; *Iranian,* by Albert J. Carnoy. Vol. 7: *African,* by Alice Werner. Vol. 10: *North American,* by Hartley B. Alexander. Vol. 12: *Egyptian,* by W. Max Müller; *Indo-Chinese,* by James G. Scott.

GURNEY, OLIVER R. *The Hittites.* London: Penguin, 1952.

HAZLITT, W. CAREW. *Faiths and Folklore of the British Isles.* 2 vols. New York: Blom, 1965.

HOOKE, SAMUEL H. *Middle-Eastern Mythology.* London: Penguin, 1968.

————, ed. *Myth, Ritual, and Kingship.* London: Oxford, 1958.

HOWE, ELLIC. *Urania's Children: The Strange World of the Astrologers.* London: Kimber, 1967.

INGLIS, STUART J. *Planets, Stars, and Galaxies.* 2nd ed. New York: Wiley, 1967.

JOBES, GERTRUDE. *Dictionary of Mythology, Folklore and Symbols.* 3 vols. New York: Scarecrow, 1961–62.

KING, LEONARD W. *Legends of Babylon and Egypt in Relation to Hebrew Tradition.* Published for the British Academy by H. Milford. London: Oxford, 1918.

KISHAUER, K. *Der Sternhimmel in Feldglas.* Leipzig: Hesse & Becker, 1928.

LANGDON, STEPHEN H. *Babylonian Epic of Creation; Restored from the . . . tablets of Assur.* Transcription, translation, and commentary. London: Oxford, 1923.

LEACH, MARIA, ed. *Standard Dictionary of Folklore, Mythology and Legend.* New York: Funk and Wagnalls, 1972.

LEO, ALAN. *Dictionary of Astrology.* Edited by Vivian E. Robson. London: "Modern Astrolgy" Office, 1929.

LILLY, WILLIAM. *Christian astrology modestly treated of in three books. The first containing the use of an ephemeris. . . .* London, 1647.

LOMAX, LEILA H. [LELA OMAR]. *Your Future: The Zodiac's Guide to Success in Life.* Philadelphia: Penn, 1904.

LUM, PETER. *The Stars in Our Heaven: Myths and Fables.* New York: Pantheon, 1948.

LYNDOE, EDWARD. *Astrology for Everyone.* Rev. ed. New York: Dutton, 1970.

MEYER, M. WILHELM. *Die Koenigin des Tages und ihr Reich.* Teschen: K. Prochaska, 1900.

MOTZ, LLOYD. *This is Astronomy.* New York: Columbia, 1963.

MUIRDEN, JAMES. *Stars and Planets.* New York: Crowell, 1965.

National Astrological Journal. Published monthly, 1933–35. Sponsored by National Astrological Association, Hollywood, Calif.

NAYLOR, P. I. *Astrology: An Historical Examination.* New York: Pergamon, 1968.

NEWCOMB, SIMON. *Popular Astronomy.* New York: Harper, 1878.

REED, ALEXANDER W. *Myths and Legends of Maoriland.* Wellington, N.Z.: Reed, 1946.

ROLFE, WILLIAM J., and GILLET, JOSEPH A. *Handbook of the Stars, for School and Home Use.* Boston: Woolworth, Ainsworth, 1870.

SANDARS, NANCY K., trans. *Epic of Gilgamesh.* London: Penguin, 1960.

SERVISS, GARRETT P. *Astronomy with an opera-glass: A popular introduction to the study of the starry heavens with the simplest of optical instruments. . . .* 3rd ed. New York: Appleton, 1890.

SEWARD, ALFRED F. *The Zodiac and Its Mysteries: A Study of Planetary Influences upon the Physical, Mental and Moral Nature of Mankind.* Chicago: Seward, 1967.

UNSÖLD, ALBRECHT. *The New Cosmos.* Translated by William H. McCrea. New York: Springer, 1969.

VAN DER WAERDEN, B. L., *History of the Zodiac.* Arch. für Orient Forschungen, 1952–53.

WHEY, A. N. *The Reading of the Stars and Those Who Love Them.*

WILDE, GEORGE, and DODSON, JOSEPH. *A Treatise of Natal Astrology.* Halifax, Yorks.: Occult, 1894.

WOOLLEY, C. LEONARD. *The Sumerians.* New York: Norton, 1965.

GLOSSARY

Aldebaran, the brightest star in the constellation Taurus.

Alexandria, famous Egyptian seaport. Known also for its excellent library.

Andromeda, an Ethiopian princess who was to be sacrificed to save her country. She was chained to a rock to be devoured by a sea monster. Perseus, son of Zeus, defeated the monster and married Andromeda. Also, the name of a constellation.

Antares, the largest and brightest star in the constellation Scorpius.

Aphrodite, Greek goddess of beauty and love.

Apis, the sacred bull worshiped by the ancient Egyptians.

Apollo, god of manly youth and beauty. Also god of music, poetry, and healing.

Argonauts, the Greeks who sailed with Jason, their leader and hero, to obtain the golden fleece.

Artemis, goddess of the moon and of the hunt. She was the twin sister of Apollo.

Asclepius (Aesculapius), the god of healing.

Astraea, goddess of justice. The last of the gods to leave the earth at the end of the Golden Age.

Astrology, the belief that the stars regulate and influence human behavior and actions; also that they influence and direct the lives of ainmals and plants.

Astronomy, the study of the stars.

Athamas, king of Thessaly, who married the phantom Nephele.

Athene, Greek goddess of wisdom and skills.

Cadmus, a prince of Phoenicia who slew a dragon and sowed its teeth in the ground. It is said that he brought the alphabet to the Greeks.

Caucasus, a region from which it is said the white race came.

Centaurs, a race of creatures half man, half horse, descendants of Ixion and living in the mountains of Thessaly.

Centaurus, a southern constellation lying between the Southern Cross and Hydra.

Chios, capital of the Greek island of Chios off the west coast of Asia Minor. Famous for its figs.

Chiron, the greatest of the Centaurs. He had knowledge of many things and the gift of prophecy.

Colchis, a kingdom on the eastern shore of the Black Sea.

Coma Berenice, the hair of Berenice, sacrificed to the goddess Aphrodite, who placed it in the sky as the tail of Leo the Lion.

Constellation, a group of fixed stars in the heaven.

Cretans, people who lived on the island of Crete.

Cronus, a Titan who ruled the universe until he was defeated by Zeus, who then became ruler himself.

Cyclops, a race of giants with one eye only, in the middle of the forehead. They are said to have lived in Sicily and were often blacksmiths.

Decans, divisions of the sky followed by the Egyptians, Chaldeans, and Greeks. They were belts of stars following each other by ten days.

Deucalion, son of Prometheus. He and his wife Pyrrha were the only survivors of the great flood. They became the ancestors of a new race.

Diana, Roman name for Artemis.

Dionysus, god of wine and the vine.

Dioscuri, the twin brothers Castor and Pollux.

Ea, ancient god of Mesopotamia. At night he was the god of the underground fresh waters.

Eos, sister of the sun god. She persuaded her brother to bring back the sight of the blind Orion.

Equinox, the two times of the year when the center of the sun crosses the equator and day and night are equal in length. The vernal (spring) equinox is around March 21 and the autumnal equinox around September 23.

Etna, volcanic mountain in Sicily.

Eurystheus, the king who gave Heracles the twelve tasks to perform.

Gilgamesh, the hero of an epic poem written before the Bible. The poem tells the story of the life of the legendary king Gilgamesh.

Hammurabi, a famous ruler of Babylonia from 2067 B.C. to 2025 B.C.

Helle, the sister of Phryxus, who was drowned in the Hellespont when she and her brother were fleeing on the ram with the golden fleece.

Hellespont, waters in which Helle fell when fleeing with her brother on the ram with the golden fleece. Now the Dardanelles.

Hera, wife of Zeus.

Heracles (Hercules), the greatest and most fearless of the Greek heroes. He could not be hurt by any weapon in any part of his body except the heel.

Hermes, a Greek god who was Zeus's messenger.

Horoscope, a way of telling fortunes by the stars.

Horus, sun god of ancient Egypt. Usually shown with the head of a hawk.

Hydra, monstrous serpent with nine heads. Some say it had more heads.

Ino, daughter of Cadmus and wife of Athamas, king of Thessaly.

Ishtar, chief goddess of the Babylonians and Assyrians. Goddess of love and fertility.

Isis, Egyptian goddess of fertility and wife of the god Osiris.

Ixion, father of the Centaurs.

Juno, Roman name for Hera.

Lemnos, an island of Greece, sacred to Vulcan.

Lerna, a swamp near Argos in Greece where the monster Hydra lived.

Libya, a country in the northern part of Africa.

Lunar, of the moon.

Macedonia, empire of ancient Greece, conquered by the Romans.

Memphis, ancient capital of Egypt.

Mayas, an ancient race of Indians living in Central America and Yucatan.

Nephele, wife of Athamas, king of Thessaly.

Nut, mother goddess of Egypt.

Nymphs, lesser Greek goddesses who lived in the rivers and springs, in the hills and among the trees.

Oracle, a place where people came for answers and advice. The answers were given by priests who questioned the gods, but were often hard to understand. The most famous was the oracle at Delphi.

Orion, a great hunter. After his death he was placed in the sky as a group of stars.

Osiris, chief god of ancient Egypt. He represented the good in life and was often identified with the river Nile.

Pan, a Greek god with legs of a goat. He was often seen playing musical pipes. He was the god of shepherds, pastures, and forests.

Phryxus, son of Athamas and Nephele.

Polydeuces, another name for Pollux.

Prometheus, one of the Titans. He stole fire from heaven and taught man how to use it.

Ptolemy, a succession of kings who ruled Egypt from 333 B.C. to 30 B.C.

Puma, a mountain lion.

Regulus, a great star in the constellation of Leo.

Samos, a Greek island.

Satyrs, gods of the woods. Their bodies were part human, part animal. They were devoted to Dionysus, god of wine and the vine.

Sea, that area of the heavens which contains Aquarius, Capricornus, and Pisces. It was the part ruled by Aquarius and was considered the great heavenly sea.

Seth, one of the sons of Nut, Egyptian mother goddess.

Sirius, dog star, said to be the brightest star in the sky.

Solar, coming from the sun.

Solstice, the two times of the year when the sun is at its greatest distance from the equator. The summer solstice is on June 21 or 22 and is the longest day of the year. The winter solstice is around December 22 and is the shortest day of the year.

Sumerians, an ancient and powerful people who lived in Mesopotamia and were famous in the cultural life of the Near East.

Themis, goddess of law and justice. She sat next to Zeus and advised him.

Titans, children of Uranus (Heaven) and Gaea (Earth). They ruled the world before Zeus, son of the Titan Cronus.

Trigon, a division of the zodiac. The four trigons, each containing three signs, represent the four elements—fire, earth, water, and air.

Typhon (Typhoeus), a monster with a hundred snake heads and a terrible voice. Slain by Zeus and buried under Mount Aetna.

Zeus, chief god of the ancient Greeks. Son of Cronus and Rhea, gods of the sky and the weather.

Zodiac (*zodiakos*), an imaginary circle or belt of animals in the Heaven consisting of twelve constellations each spaced exactly thirty degrees along the path of the sun, the moon, and the planets.